READINGS IN 2 KINGS

An interpretation arranged for Personal
and Group Bible Study

with questions and notes

READINGS IN 2 KINGS

An Interpretation arranged for Personal and Group Bible Study

with questions and notes

RONALD S. WALLACE

Eugene, Oregon

Wipf and Stock Publishers
199 W 8th Ave, Suite 3
Eugene, OR 97401

Readings in 2 Kings
An Interpretation Arranged for Personal and Group Bible Studies
By Wallace, Ronald S.
Copyright©1996 by Wallace, Ronald S.
ISBN: 1-57910-040-6
Publication date 5/30/1997

To
SHONA
and
KIRSTY-ANN

CONTENTS

Foreword   x

Acknowledgments   xi

Introduction — The Monarchy in Israel   xii
    God Gives Israel a King   xii
    Disillusionment and Hope   xiii
    I Kings — from Solomon to Ahab   xiv
    II Kings — the Unfolding Tragedy   xvi
    God — Patience, Suffering and Sovereignty   xvii
    (Note on authorship)   xix

I Elijah and Ahaziah   2 Kings 1:1–18
    Israel after Carmel   1
    A King to be Reckoned With   3
    The Fire from Heaven   6
    The Peacemaker   7
    'Go down with Him'   9
    (Notes, and Points for Further Discussion)   10

II The Ascension of Elijah   2 Kings 2:1–18
    'The Lord has sent me to the Jordan'   14
    'As they continued walking and talking'   16
    'Where is the Lord, the God of Elijah?'   19
    Reality or Imagination?   21
    (Notes, and Points for Further Discussion)   21

III Elisha Becomes Involved   2 Kings 2:19–3:27
    In Jericho   25
    At Bethel   27
    In the Campaign Against Moab   29
    (Notes, and Points for Further Discussion)   32

IV	**Elisha — On Home Ground** 2 Kings 4:1–37	
	Elisha, the Pastor	36
	With the Widow — a Sign from God	38
	With the Widow — 'Pay your debts and live'	39
	With the Shunammite — the Crisis	41
	With the Shunammite — the Questioning and the Agony	43
	(Notes, and Points for Further Discussion)	46

V	**Three Early Miracles** 2 Kings 4:38–44, 6:1–7	
	Elisha and the 'Company of Prophets'	51
	God's Grace at the 'Lower Levels of Life'	53
	From Jesus to Elisha — and Vice Versa	54
	(1) 'Death in the Pot'	55
	(2) 'Only a little for too many'	56
	(3) An accident!	58
	(Notes and Points for Further Discussion)	59

VI	**Naaman — and Gehazi** 2 Kings 5:1–27	
	Naaman — Disillusionment, Humiliation and Discovery	63
	Today — Disillusionment, Humiliation and Discovery	66
	The Sequel	68
	Elisha on the Verge of Politics	71
	(Notes and Points for Further Discussion)	72

VII	**The Terrorist Campaign** 2 Kings 6:8–23	
	An Open Door	75
	'Are there not twelve hours in a day?'	77
	The Prayer and its Answer	78
	Elisha's Moment	80
	An Incident in Pastoral Care	82
	(Notes and Points for Further Discussion)	83

VIII	**The Siege of Samaria** 2 Kings 6:24–7:20	
	Human Nature under Stress	87
	The King Reveals Himself	88
	The Waiting Church and Prophet	90

	The Word	91
	The Four Witnesses	92
	Judgment with Salvation	93
	(Notes and Points for Further Discussion)	94
IX	**The Anointing Hazael and Jehu** 2 Kings 8:1–9:13	
	Elisha — Agent of Judgment and Sign of Grace	99
	Elisha and Hazael	101
	The Task before Jehu	104
	The Anointing	105
	(Notes and Points for Further Discussion)	106
X	**Jehu**	
	2 Kings 9:14–10:36	
	The Task and the Calling	110
	The Point of Failure	112
	Yet God Sees and Accepts!	114
	True Zeal and its Vulnerability	117
	(Notes and Points for Further Discussion)	119
XI	**Judah — from Athaliah to Joash** 2 Kings 11:1–12:21	
	Athaliah Triumphant	123
	Jehosheba and Jehonadab	125
	Kindled Hope and Renewed Vision	127
	Joash — the Achievement	128
	Joash — the Final Tragedy and Shame	131
	(Notes and Points for Further Discussion)	132
XII	**The Dynasty of Jehu** 2 Kings 13:1–14:29	
	Israel after Jehu — Two Kings Turn to Prayer	136
	Israel after Jehu — Elisha is still There!	139
	Israel after Jehu — The Door of Hope is Closed.	142
	Amaziah of Judah	143
	(Notes and Points for Further Discussion)	145
XIII	**The Exile of Israel and the Decline of Judah** 2 Kings 15:1–17:41	
	Israel Rejects its Destiny	148

	Contents	ix

The Decline of the Kingdom and the Fall	
of Samaria	150
The Judas of Judah	151
'They Followed the Nations that were Around Them'	153
An 'Establishment' Compromise	156
(Notes and Points for Further Discussion)	157

XIV Hezekiah — An Intimate Portrait (i) 2 Kings 18:1–19:37

Strength in Weakness!	160
The Road of Self-discovery	163
The Sheep without a Shepherd!	165
A Cry from the Depths	166
The Word	167

XV Hezekiah — An Intimate Portrait (ii) 2 Kings 20:1–21

Again in the Depths — Sickness, Disillusionment,	
and the Fear of Death!	170
Confidence before God	171
The Struggle towards Greater Assurance	172
A Significant Lapse	175
(Notes on Chs XIV and XV and Points	
for Further Discussion)	176

XVI Josiah   2 Kings 21:1–23:30

Judah under Doom, and God under Stress!	182
Josiah — Miracle, Sign and Example	184
The Book and the Purge	186
The Final Phase — Tragedy and Failure?	189
A Labour — 'Not in Vain!'	191
(Notes and Points for Further Discussion)	193

Epilogue   2 Kings 23:31–25:30

The Narrative	198

FOREWORD

This is the second volume of two, designed to open up the Second Book of Kings so that the central thrust of its message can be appreciated by the ordinary reader.

In pursuing this aim I have tried to avoid, within the main text, too much scholarly antiquarian background material, critical grammatico-historical detail, or discussion of an expert nature. Where such discussion is helpful I have put it in added notes. The book is divided into sixteen studies which can be used from week to week by a group wishing to do continuous Bible study. The same arrangement can be found helpful for a personal study of the book. A series of questions for further thought or discussion are added to each section. The Introduction is designed to enable the reader to enter the study of this particular volume without necessarily reading the previous one.

ACKNOWLEDGMENTS

Though I have occasionally mentioned a commentary to which I have been recently indebted, nevertheless over very many years I have taken so many notes from books in so many libraries that much must be in this text without possible acknowledgment. I would like especially however to mention Jacques Ellul's *The Politics of God and the Politics of Man*. In my early ministry I was bold enough to publish a book, *Elijah and Elisha*, a series of addresses of a devotional nature which I gave from my pulpit and at conferences. It received much appreciation, and the African Christian press published a large revised edition of it for circulation there. Ellul's treatment of Elisha as an important historical figure has enabled me to discover the continuity within the stories, about him and to appreciate him as a great and shrewd statesman, a worthy successor of Elijah, and to discover richer meaning in the chapters devoted to his ministry.

The biblical text is mainly that of the New Revised Standard Version.

I am very grateful again to the Rev. Dr R. B. W. Walker for checking my references and correcting the proofs, and to my publisher Dr Douglas Grant for his kindness and help.
Edinburgh 1996.

INTRODUCTION

The Monarchy in Israel

God Gives Israel a King

During the whole period of the Judges, the structure of Israel's national life was that of a loose confederation of tribes held together by their one-family tradition, religious faith and common sense of purpose under the Lord their God. In many of the surrounding lands, however, monarchy, involving hereditary succession, seemed to be the system of government which worked best, and there were always those among the people of God who wanted to become like other nations and to adapt to such a centralised form of rule. When Gideon, for example, was approached by them to become their king, he resisted the call for such a change. 'I will not rule over you, and my son will not rule over you; the LORD will rule over you' (Judges 8:23). We can regard his answer as an inspired prophetic expression of God's will for the direction of his people. Israel was meant to remain always unique among other nations not only in the revelation of God given them through the Patriarchs and Moses, but even also in such a matter as that of their political structure. It had been God's hope that at this stage in their history they would leave it in his hand to select and raise up among them from time to time a leader of his own choice. It was his will that they should always trust him to set over them a good shepherd who would listen to his word and care for his sheep.

As time passed, however, the difficulties of remaining under such theocratic rule steadily mounted. The growing separateness of the tribes from each other led to a lack of ability to give a co-ordinated and quick response to the growing dangers around them. The majority began to want what seemed from a human point of view something more stable and protective by way of government. Their discontent became acute even under the reign of such a great leader as Samuel, and in his old age they sent a deputation to him. 'Appoint for us ... a king to govern us, like other nations' (1 Sam. 8:5).

Samuel himself grieved both over the personal insult, and the disbelief implied in their demand. God, in comforting him, also expressed his deep displeasure in their inability to trust his ways and his wisdom. But at the same time God listened to the people. He understood the stress he had been asking them to bear, and he yielded to the prayer they uttered in their weakness. Samuel himself was told to yield to their wishes, and to recognise that Saul, then an able and ardent young patriot, was the best candidate for the job, and to make arrangements to have him elected and crowned the first king of Israel.

Disillusionment and Hope

The story of the early years of the monarchy given in the two books of Samuel leaves us with both questioning and hope about the future. Even as he consented to their wishes, Samuel was inspired to remind the expectant people about the dangers ahead. Kings, he affirmed, tended to be self-willed, arrogant, greedy, proud and careless of the weak (1 Sam. 8:10–18). Saul's reign, however, began with acclaim, and he was ardently supported by a united Israel in a great victory over the Ammonites. But he soon proved unreliable, impulsive and strong-willed. His character deteriorated, and he lost his vision, faith and reason too. God had to find, and appoint a substitute for him — David!

David pleased God by the obedient trust he placed in him, his sensitive understanding of his will and his openness to his word.

There were certainly faults and sins that marred his service, especially in the Bathsheba affair, but always he was able to turn back to God in faithfulness committing himself thankfully in true and deep repentance to the punishment with which God afflicted him. At the height of his career God expressed his pleasure in his kingship, and made a covenant that he would keep a descendant of David on the throne of Israel for ever. In the great days to come, when the blessing promised to Israel at last spread to all nations (cf. Gen. 12:1–3), a great messianic king of the line of David would be there upon its throne (cf. 2 Sam. 7:8–16).

1 Kings — from Solomon to Ahab

The two books of Kings give us the history of this monarchy within Israel from the time of the death of David till its last earthly representative was dethroned at the fall of Jerusalem nearly four hundred years later. As king succeeds king it very soon becomes obvious that even in this now divinely sanctioned institution, trust in God and a love for truth and righteousness are not going to be hereditary gifts. Some of the kings obviously go their own way from the beginning of their rule. Others are shown to begin with a sincere effort to please God but fail in the long run. Moreover, the people under the monarchy are as ready to rebel against their destiny as they were under Moses in the wilderness, and seldom is even a well-intentioned king able to resist the downward trend. It is a tragic feature of the whole history that the two most godly rulers in the whole succession make their appearance, and seek to reform the establishment only after the situation has deteriorated beyond recall and God has made an irreversible decision to end the whole regime and send the nation into exile in Babylon.

It is important that the reader who begins his or her study at 2 Kings should be acquainted with the course of the history up to the beginning of this particular book.

Solomon began his career with great celebration and dedication. Signs and promises were given to him by God that his reign will be marked by hitherto unparalleled greatness. He builds a temple and is blessed. The whole world marvels at his wisdom. Then everything collapses and he ends his life in abject failure, wilful, sensual and foolish.

His personal collapse helps to bring about a division in the kingdom. There had always been tension between rival tribes, and this had already found expression in the bitter civil war between the northern tribes who supported Saul and those of the southern area, around Jerusalem which supported David. They had all united when the whole nation finally asked David to be the king, but Solomon had centralised government entirely in Jerusalem and had directed the flow of the nation's wealth to the south. His son Rehoboam was an irresponsible youth, and unable to cope with the resulting political tension. Moreover, as a sign of his displeasure with what was happening God had given his sanction to Jeroboam, a promising young leader from the north to set up a second kingdom there among the disaffected tribes.

It is in his account of the setting up and development of this Northern kingdom (now called the kingdom of Israel in contrast to the kingdom of Judah) that the writer of Kings begins to show us how kings can become perverse as well as weak, and how willingly and easily his people can be led astray. Jeroboam disappointed God more quickly and more deliberately than even Solomon had done. As soon as he was given his power, he ensured that the religion of his people would not in any way interfere with his own political aims. He gave way to the fear that if he allowed his people, as was their custom, to visit Jerusalem to worship the Lord, he would ultimately lose their loyalty. He therefore built two temples within his realm, one at Bethel and the other at Dan, rivals to that at Jerusalem. He set up in each sanctuary the image of a golden calf, proclaiming that these represented 'your gods, O Israel, who brought you out of the land of Egypt' (1 Kings 12:28). Moreover, he appointed prophets of his own to support his alien religious set-up. It is to be noted that the sin of making such a graven image to represent him, caused God's continuing anger. He patiently held on to this people of the North, and tried to win them back to himself. After all, they were offspring of Abraham, and heirs to the promise. Yet neither they nor their kings eventually repented of this sin or destroyed these images. So vicious in God's sight was this practice that again and again it is cited as the main reason why they were finally sent into exile under the King of Assyria, a hundred and fifty years before the fall of Jerusalem.

Jeroboam's own royal house soon collapsed after he died. One or two bloody revolutions almost wiped out his kingdom. A strong leader, Omri, however, was able to take control, claim the throne, stabilise the kingdom, build a capital city called Samaria, and set up a new and much more lasting dynasty. He married his son Ahab to Jezebel, the daughter of the neighbouring kingdom of Tyre.

Ahab went beyond even Jeroboam in perfidy. He came completely under the power of his wife allowing her to build a temple for her pagan god Baal in Samaria. Baal was the traditional God of the land around them. His worship, at his many hill shrines, was believed to bring fertility and involved sexual prostitution. Such worship being given official status became a serious threat to what remained of the truth of God as revealed to Israel at Sinai. Jezebel's daughter Athaliah was married to the contemporary king of Judah, and Baalism took a firm and threatening grip of the minds and affections of people in both kingdoms.

II Kings — *The Unfolding Tragedy*
The unfolding story, as given in the text now before us is marked by deepening tragedy. Baalism is certainly overcome by the grace of God, the power of his word, and the marvellously effective ministry of the prophets. The weakness of the kings in their office is, however, all the more fully exposed. Most of them fail as they are fully tested. In Israel Ahaziah proves even more reprobate than his father Ahab. Jehoram proves as unreliable. Hope for the future of the nation is temporarily raised by the effect of the zeal of Jehu and the extraordinary piety of Jehoahaz and Jehoash. The writer, indeed, at this point in the history refers hopefully to the prosperity with which God begins to bless them as Jeroboam II comes to the throne. He assures us that God had never yet pronounced any final sentence of condemnation on Israel. But all hope for this people is finally crushed by the crude opportunism of Jeroboam II, who grossly abuses the resources of wealth and power opened up for him by God's mercy. He finds the majority of those around him only too ready to support his callous and atheistic regime. We are not surprised that the dynasty of Jehu soon collapses and the kingdom of the North moves on to its doom.

As we follow the history of the Judah, we have to remember that the final drift of affairs was determined as much by the way the people themselves responded to the law and word of their prophets, as by the decisions and behaviour of the king himself. A comparatively good king tended to be resisted, a king disobedient to God tended to be popular. Ominous signs that Judah had no greater stability than Israel appear quite early. Joash, after a career of great promise, and Amaziah, after one of great folly, are both murdered by their subjects. They are followed by Azariah (or Uzziah) and Jotham who do their best, but each has within his record a 'nevertheless'. Neither attained to the hope of God for a truly worthy son of David. Then comes Ahaz, zealous to surpass in wickedness even the worst kings who sealed the doom of the kingdom of Israel, and defiant in his admiration of everything that displeased the Lord. It was inevitable that Judah as a monarchy, under a series including such as Ahaz, Manasseh, Jehoiakim and Zedekiah should finally head for destruction.

God — Patience, Sorrow and Sovereignty
We are meant as we read through the whole story to notice the patience and hope that God himself continually shows. He makes his decision to change his hoped-for plan only long after its hopelessness had become obvious.

There was always a willingness to postpone what was beginning to seem inevitable, and finally deep regret in his very decision to bring his plan to an end. Even when individual kings come far short of his requirements, they are praised for whatever virtue they show, and he is always there ready to offer grace and strength to any who are willing to turn to him. It is one of the brightest features of the Book of Kings that in the midst of the doom-laden series of rogues who bring about the collapse of Judah, there should appear Hezekiah and Josiah, best by far of all the sons of David. They came too late to change the impending direction of history and their ways and aims were ultimately rejected by the will of the people. Yet their prayers were answered and they were accorded for a time brilliant success in their efforts for the kingdom. There can be no doubt moreover that when the exiles in Babylon were seeking understanding, comfort and guidance in the midst of the perplexities and suffering, they would find themselves inspired by these two examples. It would stand out in their memory that, as in the case of Hezekiah, God's strength can be made perfect in human weakness, and as with Josiah, stubborn adherence to the Word of God can never be in vain.

It is in the book of Jeremiah that we have a touching expression of God's sorrow and disappointment over the failure of his plan for Israel under the monarchy. At some point during the years 587–6 BC in which Jerusalem was being attacked and destroyed, Baruch, the young secretary of the prophet complained that God was making things too hard for him to bear. He had, of course, already suffered much under the public contempt and persecution which had come to him as he had witnessed for God alongside his master. And now, finding no relief during the final judgment that was falling on the city — the evictions, the burnings, the rapes and the enslavement, that were taking place all around him — he expressed his feelings of frustration to God. 'Woe is me,' he cried, 'the Lord has added sorrow to my pain; I am weary with my groaning, and I feel no rest.' God immediately sent him an answer through Jeremiah: 'Thus says the Lord, I am going to break down what I have built and pluck up what I have planted — that is the whole land. And you, do you seek great things for yourself?' (Jer. 45:3–5). Was Baruch not now in a position to understand God's *own* personal and bitter disappointment? There is, further, in the Book of Ezekiel an expression of the determination of God that in future he alone would be king over Israel and that never again would he leave the opportunity open to them to become like other nations (Ezek. 20:32–33).

Since the shortcomings of the Old Covenants which God made with Israel, especially of that which he made with David and his heirs, had become so exposed (cf. Heb. 8:7–8), God brought about the exile. He set in motion an entirely new plan in order to fulfil his purpose with this nation. They were to be punished and disciplined. They had to be made to understand the folly and hopelessness of their old ways in the midst of long-drawn-out suffering and bitter shame. But he himself would be working with them, teaching them, healing their souls and wounds, so that in and through their sorrow and their renewed grasp of his love they could be brought to true repentance and start again. He gave them through the prophet Jeremiah the promise of a new start in which old things would pass away, and all things become new. He would meet their need by bringing about in their heart a new creation. It would all come to pass in the latter days when he would deal with them under a new covenant (Jer. 31:31-34).

The reader is meant to ponder over the editorial comment added to the book years after it was issued. In the thirty-seventh year of his captivity king Jehoiachin who had been taken into exile by Nebuchadnezzar, was brought out of prison, and given exalted status in the court of Babylon. He was the rightful heir to the throne of David, and the heir to the promises that had been made to him. Even though God had destroyed the monarchy in Israel, he had not gone back on what he had spoken. 'The days are surely coming, says the Lord, when I will raise up for David a righteous Branch and he shall reign as king and deal wisely, and shall execute justice and righteousness in the land' (Jer. 23:5, cf. 33:14).

Note on Authorship
Who was responsible for the writing, editing and issuing this book, and when did it finally appear? One suggestion is that it was written by Jeremiah. Another that we owe it to a group of scholars and thinkers who were in Babylon during the exile. The book itself tells us about the sources available at the time, from which the author or authors could have taken either information or quotations such as e.g. the *Acts of Solomon* (1 Kings 11:41), and his references indicate that there were many such annals then in circulation, or in official archives about the reigns of kings available for those who desired extra information. It seems reasonable to think of a single author as being responsible for the work about the time of the exile, and, of sections being later added (e.g. 2 Kings 24:27-30),and possible editing undertaken, after the first issue.

Obviously the writer regarded the teaching of the book of Deuteronomy as of great importance. It dwells on such subjects as the dangers of misrule by a king, the ideals he should follow, the significance of the temple, and the perils of false worship. The writer of this book often can quote it at great length. He saw that the future of Israel was to be determined by whether it inherited the blessings promised in it for obedience to its laws, or the curses threatened for disobedience (Deut. 28). One of its most important laws, in his eyes, was that there should be only one centre of worship in the land (Deut. 12). It was by each king's obedience or disobedience to such teaching in this book that he finally classified them, towards the end of his account of each, as good or bad.

His constant reference to, and application of, the teaching of the book of Deuteronomy, however, need not dominate our reading of the book as we seek to find out what it has to say to us today. Within the unfolding of the history we enter a world of story, about persons like ourselves in situations that we can easily match with our own today, struggling as we ourselves have to do with the question of whether or not, and how, to obey the word of God.

CHAPTER I

ELIJAH AND AHAZIAH
2 Kings 1:1–18

The Narrative

Shortly after he became King of Israel, Ahaziah, the eldest son of Ahab, was seriously injured in an accident. Instead of turning to the Lord he sent messengers to inquire at the shrine of Baalzebub. This was a public sign that he was prepared to resist the reforms brought in by Elijah the prophet, and to support the Baal religion of his mother, Jezebel. An angel of the Lord commanded Elijah to accost the messengers and pronounce a sentence of death on the King. Ahaziah reacted by sending soldiers to take him captive. After the fire from heaven, called down by Elijah in mistaken zeal, destroyed the first two companies, an appeal from the officer in charge of the third went home to the distraught prophet, persuaded him to face the King, and deal with him in person.

Israel after Carmel

The brief mention, at the beginning of this chapter, that '*after the death of Ahab, Moab rebelled against Israel*', is meant to be taken by us as an indication that the international strength and prestige of both this little nation, Israel, and its sister kingdom, Judah, was beginning to wane. Two generations ago, under Omri, Israel had partially recovered the political strength and influence it had under David. King Ahab, the son of Omri, in spite of his faults and disastrous rule at home, had been among other nations a force to be reckoned with.

Now, however, as we follow the narrative of 2 Kings, we will find ourselves entering a phase of Middle-East history in which both Israel and Judah, instead of being able to indulge any more in petty colonialism among weaker neighbours, will themselves become vassal states of the now developing great empires, Assyria and Babylon, finally to be almost swallowed up by both of them.

As we read through the rest of this chapter, however, international affairs are entirely forgotten, and we are reminded of the internal religious and political struggle within the Kingdom of Israel. That struggle was taking place between, on the one hand the prophets of the Lord under the leadership of Elijah, and on the other hand, the religion of Baal which had been recently imported into Israel especially by Jezebel, the domineering wife of Ahab. She had gone the length of building a temple for Baal in the capital city, Samaria. Prophets of the Lord had been killed, and Baalism had been allowed to take firm hold of the imagination and the natural instincts of the people. We can understand why they found the new creed attractive. The old Covenant religion dominated by the Ten Commandments and Moses, had itself been perverted by generations of false teaching and in the form in which it was then taught had lost much of its distinctive power and reality (see note). Baalism seemed to offer something less artificial and more exciting. Baal was the traditional god of the land and of each Canaanite locality. He always had his goddess alongside of him. He was easy going, and easy to worship. All the surrounding pagan nations believed that their own fertility, and that of their lands and herds, depended on his sexual prowess, and their worship of him at the countless hill-shrines around, involved rites that were designed to stimulate him.

By the time our chapter opens, however, God had already intervened decisively to break the hold of this newly established idolatry over his people. He had raised up Elijah the Prophet to announce a famine (1 Kings 17). This was to prove that it was he and not Baal who controlled the climate and watered the earth (1 Kings 17). He had marvellously supported Elijah in his dramatic encounter with the whole priesthood of Baal on Mount Carmel (1 Kings 18). There the fire had fallen from heaven only in answer to Elijah's prayer to the God of Abraham,

Isaac and Jacob. The emptiness and fraudulence of Baal religion had been decisively exposed, the pagan priesthood had been slaughtered, and the great mass of the people had fallen on their faces to the ground, in repentance, confessing that the Lord, alone, was God.

What happened at Carmel changed the religious balance of power in Israel. Public opinion moved decisively to the side of the old religion of the Covenant. Elijah became the dominant figure in the background of the nation's life, and the prophets of the Lord were free to speak his word, give counsel, and intervene in national affairs. Yet Baalism became a still-powerful underground movement and, as the Naboth affair showed (1 Kings 21), it continued for nearly a generation to do severe damage here and there to what was traditional in Israel's life. Moreover, through the marriage of Jezebel's daughter into the royal house of Judah (2 Kings 8:18) it became a powerful influence in that Kingdom too. Elijah realised at Horeb (1 Kings 19) that there would have to be a long wait for the political situation to develop before it was finally extirpated.

It is against this background, and from the scant information given to us in this chapter, that we have to make an estimate of the character of the young King Ahaziah.

A King to be Reckoned With

What we immediately read of Ahaziah's early days on his throne gives us an unflattering first impression of his character — especially if we compare him with what has just been told us of Ahab his father. The latter when he found the integrity of his Kingdom under threat from Aram immediately made war, sustained a mortal wound on the battlefield, and died with honour (1 Kings 22). With the prestige and pride of his country no less at stake through the threat and insult which had come from Moab, Ahaziah is seen rather to busy himself with repairs and readjustments to his elaborate palace windows, and to sustain a fatal injury with a fall from a balcony.

As we read on, however, we are soon undeceived, and we are forced to admire him for a striking and solitary display of the kind of moral courage which his father completely lacked.

Even at this extreme crisis his life, and knowing well that he would incur the anger of Elijah and the militant moral majority who had so recently taken over public opinion and political power in his country, he took his stand firmly (as his father had never been able to do with any consistency) on the burning religious question. He was not ashamed to declare openly the idolatry that had been deeply inbred within him by his mother Jezebel. He selected one of the Baal family of gods to whom his mother was so devoted. He knew where to find him, and he sent messengers to seek his counsel. Would he die or could he live? No effort was made to conceal the deputation or the purpose for which it was sent. The young king was thus not only declaring before the whole nation what he believed in, but also making a defiant gesture of opposition to those then in control of his nation.

It was the reaction of Elijah that finally brought out the full strength of his defiance. The prophet sent a message: '*Is it because there is no God in Israel that you are sending to inquire of Baal-zebub, the god of Ekron?* (v. 5). It was the same kind of challenge to the new king, as he had made to the people of Carmel when he had won them over (1 Kings 18:21). Had Ahaziah thought it out? And a threat of doom was added, '*You shall not leave the bed to which you have gone, but shall surely die*'. The word was sent in the hope that the King would change his mind. Ahab his father had once repented when he had heard such a verdict (1 Kings 21:27-29).

It was a severe shock to the waiting prophet to find that, instead of evident submission, he himself was suddenly faced again with the same contemptuous threat to his own life as had put him to flight after Carmel (1 Kings 19:2-3). We can imagine the young king's thoughts about the whole situation in which he found himself. He knew about Carmel (he may have been there as a child!). He knew about the famine, the fire from heaven, and the spectacular effect of Elijah's remarkable appeal for repentance. Yet he had decided that Elijah was an imposter and that the debacle at Carmel had been the result of a piece of trickery. He had become firmly persuaded that what people like Elijah held sacred —all this talk about 'men of God' and the 'Word of the Lord' was phoney. He did not believe that he himself was in any danger from the mere spoken threat of such an imposter. Moreover, with undaunted wisdom and tenacity he had prepared himself for the emergency. He had around him in his court at least a hundred men whom he could trust to seize even a prophet of the Lord, most of them reliable Baal loyalists. They were well versed in the words they were to speak when they made their arrest, and they confidently put themselves into the act as they gave '*the king's order*'. Their address to the prophet, '*O man of God*' was to be spoken in contemptuous mockery. Elijah will now learn that the word of Ahaziah is more effective than any word of the Lord!

Especially today, as we are becoming acutely aware of the power and sinister nature of the forces in our society opposing the Gospel, this story has relevance. What is the origin of evil? What is sin? There are those who would define it simply as '"breaking" of the law' or as a 'missing of the mark', and preachers have been sometimes apt to condemn simply its expression in the forms of uncontrolled sensuality, brutality, greed, or lack of love and social concern. We must not forget that we are closer to discovering its essence and understanding its true nature, when our thought about it takes full account of how it appeared in Ahaziah — as an absurd perversity of mind and will, in contempt of the truth and God, held with a pride and unashamedness that can take the form of courage. We will see that same pride and courage, apparently inconquerable, embodied in both Jezebel and Athaliah as they go each to her death. We must remind ourselves that sin can take the form of virtue. It can clothe itself in beauty. Milton made Satan appear as if there was some truly admirable nobility in his character. We must remind ourselves that what is alien to God would not be so deadly and damaging to true goodness if it did not possess such counterfeit qualities. The New Testament reminds us that the Devil can appear as an 'angel of light' (2 Cor. 11:14). Was it not in this form and with this apparent stature that Jesus had to encounter it during his wilderness temptation?

This story has relevance, too, in reminding us of its extraordinary resilience. Exposed, overcome, and under the final death-sentence that was passed on it at Calvary, it will be still here to threaten us, and to work its havoc where it is allowed, until the end of the age. When we ourselves think we have put on the whole armour God, and resisted on every front, the struggle is never over. It is as severe a continuing test to 'stand firm' after we think we have overcome (Eph. 6:13). We will find that Elijah in his day had to learn this simple lesson too.

The Fire from Heaven

The disciples of Jesus interpreted Elijah's cry, '*let fire from heaven come down and consume you and your fifty*' (v. 10) as arising out of a desire for revenge (cf. Luke 9:51–56). We do better if we find our clue to his behaviour at this juncture in the word of the Angel '*do not be afraid of him*' (v. 15). After years of undisturbed security Elijah had imagined that never again would he be faced with such virulent opposition as he had met from Jezebel, after Carmel. He was therefore completely unprepared in his mind to deal with the situation, and was acting under sudden shock. His cry to God was one of sheer panic, like that of Peter when, walking on the sea, he became suddenly aware of the strength of the waves and the wind and found himself beginning to sink.

We have to condemn Elijah, however, for giving vent to such an utterance at that moment. He let down his cause and gave a false witness to God's nature and power. Some of those who were slaughtered were undoubtedly his sworn enemies, but some may have been there simply because they were soldiers assigned this particular job that day. Moreover he had forgotten what God had taught him at Horeb: sending fire from heaven was not the only or even the best means at his disposal! Yet we have to recognise that his prayer was a cry of genuine faith uttered out of the heart of the panic. His concern was not simply for his own life but for the cause to which he had already given his life. He was deeply provoked by the insults and contempt that had been shown to the name of the Lord. His memory immediately went back to Carmel when God heard his cry and saved Israel by sending the fire. He put himself and his cause in the hands of God again in the immediate and momentary outgoing of his heart towards him. We can liken him to the old man in Psalm 71:

'O God, from my youth you have taught me,
and I still proclaim your wondrous deeds!
So even to old age and grey hairs,
O God do not forsake me,
until I proclaim your might to all the generations to come'
  (vv. 17–18, cf. also vv. 1, 5–6).

He called for God's answer in public, in face of his enemy, in complete confidence, that he would be heard. 'Those who honour me', the Lord had said, 'I will honour!' (1 Sam. 2:30).

Here was a conflict from which God himself could not stand apart, even if Elijah his servant may have failed to have been fully in touch with his mind in his praying and in his actions. God is concerned to establish truth, righteousness and love on this earth. He is willing to become involved in the earthly battles which are fought to maintain these ideals, and will take a side in such battles (Psalm 124:2, 3). So great is his concern and grace that he will support the best side, even though those on that side fail to show perfect love, and have no monopoly of truth and righteousness. God does not stand neutral when the advance of his kingdom is at stake. Therefore, he stood by Elijah when he called down the fire.

Elijah's example is, of course, not held before us here for our imitation. We do well to remember that Jesus 'rebuked' the disciples for wanting to do likewise, adding the warning 'you do not know what spirit you are of' (Luke 9:55 margin). Yet we ourselves who have felt called to serve God in the struggle against evil powers are often mistaken. We act foolishly, and we wonder if God can still use us. God is not ashamed to give his alliance to his people. If he honoured Elijah in those far-off days by sending fire from heaven, then in spite of our inadequacy and our misunderstanding of his purposes today, he will not cause us to be ashamed.

The Peacemaker

God found in the captain of the third 'fifty', the man who could bring sanity and reason into this tragic and stupid situation. Though enlisted among the pagan king's trusted bodyguard, he, like Obadiah in the court of Ahab (cf. 1 Kings 18:1—16), revered the Lord greatly. He was one of the 'seven thousand' in Israel who had not bowed the knee to Baal (1 Kings 19:18). Perhaps in fear and trembling, at the court, he had already volunteered to make a different approach to Elijah, reasoning with the king that he was wasting his manpower uselessly by continuing his policy of defiance. It is possible in any case that Ahaziah by this time was ready to enlist any one of his officers who was willing to volunteer for a most dangerous job. It is, however, the effect he had on Elijah rather than on Ahaziah, that we are told about.

In the task he was given, he was in a situation similar to that of Abigail when she heard news that David, blazing with anger and with a band of determined men were on their way to her homestead to kill her husband because of his insulting behaviour. She did not hesitate to put herself at risk, blocked David's path, and pled with him as a man of God to pause and think over the mood he was in, and the plan in his mind, which would destroy his own reputation. How foolish of him to allow passion rather than reason to lead him on! David listened, and relented, and thanked God that he had sent her to save him from the folly of his own way, 'Blessed be your good sense, and blessed be you, who have kept me today from bloodguilt', he said to her (1 Sam. 25:33).

In dealing with the situation facing him this third captain likewise put himself at risk. He had no firm guarantee that his approach would bring about any change in the mood of this now awesome prophet of the Lord. He must have believed firmly that he was in the hand and service of God in attempting what he did, and he must have prayed for the courage to make the right approach and the tact to speak the effective word. It is to be regarded as a sheer miracle that he achieved the breakthrough and opened up the whole situation so that God's work could now be seen to be done.

Elijah must have recognised that the whole tone of the approach was now different from before. It is likely that he heard in the man's plea for mercy a gentle reproach from God for forgetting that all men are not his enemies and that human lives are dear to himself: '*O man of God, please let my life, and the life of these fifty servants of yours, be precious in your sight*' (v. 13). It is likely, too, that he took to heart the powerful plea to '*look*' (v. 14) again at the devastation his fire had brought, with its destructive power! His chief service, however, was that in cooling Elijah's passion and pleading with him to think again, he opened his ear to the voice of the angel who must have been there from the very beginning of the tragic incident waiting till he would listen: '*Go down with him: do not be afraid of him.*'

When we read of this nameless man we cannot help thinking of Jesus' beatitude: 'Blessed are the peacemakers, for they will be called the children of God' (Matt. 5:9).

We need not interpret his words as a call to become an expert at counselling, or to take up such a career amid all the complexities of living together today. They are, rather, a challenge to ordinary Christian people to be prepared to step in, and as prayerfully and tactfully as they can, take what action is open to them when the peace which God means to prevail amongst families, friends and cultural associations or in neighbourhoods or even churches, is endangered. The simple story of this third captain suggests that even we ourselves might at times be given the words and the skill for such a task.

'Go down with him'

The story suggests that Elijah had been originally meant not only to send a message to the king but to hold himself in readiness to go and give him counsel. He had instead withdrawn himself to some hilltop retreat. Perhaps he had been concerned to maintain the dignity of his office. Perhaps he had come to regard the Word of God as being always chiefly political in its relevance and had thought of Ahaziah merely as representing an alien political and religious force. Perhaps at this time of his life he was tempted to give way to tiredness or fear.

He should, however, have recognised from the very beginning that his duty as a prophet in the tragic situation facing this young king demanded not the sending of an offhand distant condemnation but the approach of a pastor. Even though the message might have to end in condemnation here was an opportunity with an individual in dire need. As a representative of the Lord who loved this sinful man, he was meant to be there in person. Let him now go and speak his word face to face with the wounded king.

The angel, of course, was mildly rebuking Elijah and recalling to his mind a lesson which he already would have learned well from his own experience. It was at Carmel that he had with magnificent success called down the fire from heaven. But at Horeb the special message had come to him that God preferred to confront people in quieter and even more impressive ways. After the fire there had come 'a sound of sheer silence' (1 Kings 19:12) and when he had heard it he had covered his face, because in that strange and gentle presence he had felt as never before the nearness and the power of the living Lord. Let him learn now, again, that even in this apparently hopeless case before him, that facing the most important issue in human life, God desired to have a shepherd of his sheep there in person, in close, quiet, even pleading, encounter and was more ready to rejoice in repentance than to pronounce judgment.

This gentle rebuke of the angel is an important final feature of this story. Preaching from the pulpit is important. The majesty and justice of God must be often clearly proclaimed. The public, political and social implications of the Gospel are important and the pulpit can be effectively used to stir people into activity, protest and change. But how important it is that exactly the same man whom God has called to be his prophet should also week by week 'go down' among the people he preaches to, and that in him and in many ordinary Christians there should be this 'passion for souls' that God and his angel looked for in Elijah!

Notes

On the Difficulty Presented by this Story
The interpretation given here of this incident has assumed that the same God whom we know in Christ, with his unchanging purpose of love, was there in the midst of his people throughout the Old Testament history, revealing

himself, and seeking to open their minds to the full truth of his nature. The revelation he was seeking to give them of himself had, however, from the beginning, to struggle with their natural human blindness and overcome their slowness to respond. Even though God chose from among his people witnesses and teachers such as Moses and Elijah whom he specially inspired and instructed, even these prophets at times failed, as we see Elijah do in this instance. The truth which God was always seeking to impart could be only gradually and progressively grasped. The men and women of whom we read in the Biblical stories, and the writers of the stories themselves, were therefore always learning about God, and sometimes failed badly in their understanding of him.

Yet each story itself, in spite of its possible inadequacy to reflect the full New Testament teaching on certain points, has its own important message to bring us. No story such as this one should be ignored or rejected.

The reader should also remember that at this time in their history, the people of God did not yet share our modern concern about the sanctity and importance of each individual personal life. This was another of these points at which God, when he chose them, had to take and deal with them where they were in order to educate them. The early thought of Israel on this matter tended to take it for granted that each individual member of a community or family had a responsible share in its common guilt or sin. The sons and daughters of Achan, for example, were punished for his sin (Josh. 7:24). Though the law in Deuteronomy (24:16) taught otherwise, it was followed only on exceptional occasions (2 Kings 14:6), and it was not till the exile that the truth on this matter, which is so important to ourselves, was most clearly expressed (cf. Ezekiel 18).

The difficulty presented by the miraculous element in this story is addressed on pp. 46–48

On the Perversion of the Cult in Israel
When the united Kingdom split in two Jeroboam desired to prevent the people of the Northern tribes from travelling South to Jerusalem for worship. He therefore introduced into each of the Northern sanctuaries, at Bethel and Dan, the image of a golden calf which he persuaded the people to accept as a

representation of the 'gods of their fathers' who had brought them out of Egypt (1 Kings 12:28). He appointed prophets to support this departure from tradition. It was inevitable that from this time on, important features that were an essential aspect of God's self-revelation to his people should become obscured.

On the Word of God and History

As we read through the story we are made aware of the accidental nature of the injury that caused the death of the young king, and of the serious faults that marred the behaviour and witness of the prophet Elijah, yet it is affirmed that 'the *king died according to the Word of the Lord that Elijah had spoken* (v. 17). The word uttered by Elijah (v. 4) is shown in the midst of all these other accidental and unfortunate happenings to take control of Elijah and bring about its own fulfilment.

Points for Further Thought and Discussion

Can you think of instances in which non-believers, or opponents of the Gospel, put us to shame by the courageous way in which they make their views known. Can we learn from their example? Why are we often so backward?

Do we take the reality and power of evil seriously enough today? Can you suggest ways in which Satan today 'disguises' himself as an angel of light (2 Cor. 11:14)?

God is shown here to support, and answer, Elijah even though he was very much at fault. Why did he do so? Under what conditions, and for what reasons, does he support us in emergencies and answer our prayers today?

How should we ourselves respond today to Jesus' offer of 'blessing' to the 'peacemakers'? Can any of us go through life without being called upon to play this role? Can you think of definite circumstances in which you have, or have failed, or might be called upon, to become a peacemaker?

Think of how Jesus, the Good Shepherd often spoke of his task as saving individual souls, and is described in the Gospels as concentrating on helping individuals. Does our following of him, and our Church work today adequately reflect this aspect of his ministry?

Chapter II

THE ASCENSION OF ELISHA
2 Kings 2:1–18

The Narrative

Elijah was setting out with Elisha on a regular visit to some of the companies of prophets in the Jordan area. Suddenly under divine impulse, he feels constrained to bypass the settlements, and to move towards the river Jordan. Elisha and some of the prophets recognise that God is impelling the old man on this journey. Elisha refuses to be parted from him, and a company of prophets follow to witness what happens. One of the most mysterious and fascinating incidents in Old Testament story takes place.

'The Lord has sent me to the Jordan'

In the great early days in his ministry the 'Word of the Lord' had come to Elijah, sending him on the move, first to Cherith (1 Kings 17:3), then to Zarephath (1 Kings 17:8), then to Carmel (1 Kings 18:1), each time in anticipation of some revelation that was to be given to him, or some task to be done. Finally he had felt himself impelled to make the long journey to Horeb to wait for the final splendid word at the mouth of the cave (1 Kings 19:11). Now in his old age, the same certainty came to him that God had some new task for him to do, and some fresh revelation to give to him, and he was impelled to move on to where it was to happen. He must have realised, when it came, that the impulse might have something to do with his approaching death.

In his old age he had decided no longer to live and do his work in isolation and possibly under the influence of Elisha had begun to associate more with the younger generation of prophets who lived together in various local communities near the Jordan. It is implied in this way that he at times accompanied Elisha as he went around such companies of prophets. It was quite suddenly on one of these rounds, early one day, that the impulse came to break the routine and obey only the leading of the Spirit. He was not sure of the exact direction in which he was meant to move. At first he thought of Gilgal as the place, then of Jericho, then finally, with absolute certainty it came: *'The Lord has sent me to the Jordan'* (v, 6).

He had difficulty in reconciling himself to the fact that God was going to involve others in what was about to happen. Often hitherto, when he had been so guided, God had taken him apart from society, and had spoken to him alone. Now, especially facing death, he felt an additional impulse to be by himself. But he found that Elisha felt as divinely constrained to keep in touch with him as he himself was to move on. Moreover, on the circuitous route they had to take, they discovered that groups of the disciples themselves had become gripped by the conviction that God was about to speak some final last word to Israel through the great prophet that day. A company of these disciples felt themselves impelled to follow their two leaders at a distance so that they might witness what was to happen. Undoubtedly by the time they had reached the river Elijah had fully accepted that it was God's will to have onlookers, and Elisha at his side.

Since he never came back to tell how his mind was prompted to act, we are inevitably left to speculate about his thoughts as he halted by the river. He was now beginning to understand that the stage was now set before him to speak through miracle a final word to God's people. The waters of the river must have seemed to him like the waters of death that he now felt himself soon to pass through. The conviction came to cross it. He felt assured that as the Lord had enabled him to give a triumphant testimony to his presence and power at Carmel, he would not allow him to be ashamed as he was now called on to speak this final word to those whom he had gathered there and then to be his witnesses.

The action he took was inspired by his memories of the great leaders of Israel who had always been his inspiration and whose actions he had in previous days tried to copy. He thought of Joshua, dividing this river to enter the promised land — was he too not now facing another promised land? He thought of Moses holding out his rod over the waters that had to be rolled back if God's way were to be taken. He had no rod but he had already taken off his mantle to give it in farewell to Elisha. He struck the water with the mantle and the way opened up for him to go over.

To the witnesses standing far off, this happening was surely meant to stand within Israel's history as a sign that God himself could be there guiding and upholding his people as they went through the valley of the shadow of death (see note). Even today along with so much else in the Gospel to assure us, the Christian soul can take comfort in the imagery it inspires:

> 'When I tread the verge of Jordan,
> Bid my anxious fears subside;
> Death of death, and hell's destruction,
> Land me safe on Canaan's side.'

This was all the witnesses saw, but Elijah at this time knew that Elisha was to go on with him for he kept hold of the mantle and must have beckoned the young prophet to follow.

'As they continued walking and talking'

On the other side of Jordan the two of them were soon far beyond the sight of the fifty witnesses, and it is to the testimony of Elisha alone that we owe the account of what then followed. He must have told the story often. What he alone now witnessed was meant also to have an important place in the tradition of the people of God. Moreover his own experience there and then had a decisive part in shaping and inspiring his own later ministry. Years before, when Elijah had come to him in the field of his father's homestead and laid his mantle on his shoulders he had been called to be a prophet. But that had proved so far to be no more than a symbolic gesture, and he had had no convincing sign that God was equipping him for his task. But on this day when the prophet's mantle at last fell from heaven at his feet he realised that his call had come not simply from Elijah but from heaven. The whole experience was now to lift him up to a new, living and transforming personal relationship with God, to enlarge his vision and enlighten his mind, and thus to bring authority and power into a ministry that had hitherto lacked conviction and reality.

The talk he now had with Elijah played an important part in this sudden prophetic formation. It could have been a lengthy conversation of which we have here only the barest summary — but even that is profound and instructive. Everything hinged on the task he would have to face when he was left alone. Elijah, with his mind on the future of the cause to which he had devoted his life-work, was deeply concerned. We can read his thoughts. Was this man really fit? Had he an adequate vision of the issues at stake and the glory of the cause? Had he himself not failed to be his father in God, and were there any last minute words he must speak to help to make amends? He wanted Elisha to give him some leading clue so that he could tell him what was to matter most in the task that now faced him. '*Tell me what I may do for you, before I am taken from you*' (v. 9).

Elisha gave him the opportunity he wanted. The younger man was possessed by a need he felt for the power and fullness of the Spirit of God. Elijah, he believed, had been able to take effective and decisive action, to overcome opposition, to bring about national renewal, to maintain a burning zeal for God's cause all his days because he had been in possession of an inward power from God. Would not he too become able to say and do like things, to show the same courage; endure the same danger and persecution if he himself, a much weaker man, could inherit from him '*a double share of your spirit*' (v. 9, see note)?

The older man's reply '*You have asked a hard thing*' reflects his perplexity over the answer. Reviewing his own life, he felt that what had mattered most in his ministry had not been any sense of inward power or of being in possession of the Spirit. It had been rather his vision of the God who had shown himself to him, and the greatness of the purpose God had called him to serve. The inspiration of all he had attempted, and the strength that had seen him through everything he had achieved, had come from the word he had heard spoken to him again and again by the One whose realm had always remained above and beyond this earth. Elisha must begin to grasp this! He would never become effective, or endure the sufferings of his ministry as a prophet of God, unless he, too, was first of all, and above all, able to have this same prophetic vision and experience. He prayed that before their final parting came, God might reveal more clearly to his young friend where he had to look for the source of the strength which could alone bring about change and renewal in this corrupt and decaying world. The thought suddenly came to him that God had already begun to meet his concern and answer his prayer. What was soon to happen — the vision of his own coming ascension and the open heavens — was intended not just to be the end of his own career but a new starting point for the mission of Elisha himself. When it happened he would receive all the inspiration of mind, thought and heart that would enable him to be a true man of God. All Elijah needed to do was to alert him to be watchful. '*If you see me as I am being taken from you, it will be granted you; if not, it will not*' (v.10). We are reminded of Jesus' Baptism. The Spirit which endowed him with all the power he needed to fulfil every aspect of the ministry that lay before him, came upon him as he looked up and saw the heavens open, and heard God's voice from there. (Mark 1:9–11).

How important the power to see what is beyond the range of ordinary human understanding and vision becomes in the teaching of the New Testament! The good news proclaimed by Jesus to his disciples from the beginning of his ministry was that the Kingdom of God, the heavenly realm, was here and now in their midst (Mt. 4:17). He not only gave evidence of its presence and power in his miracles (Luke 11:20) but he prayed that his disciples would be given the power to see as well as enter it, and he urged them to seek and prize this divinely given insight (Mt. 13:16), for only as they were inspired by such vision could they be in contact with such power.

We must not of course forget, at the same time, that this power to 'see' is itself the gift of the Spirit. Joel had already prophesied that the gift of the Spirt from above would bring with it the power to 'see visions' (Joel 2:28), and the central theme of Peter's sermon on this text on the day of Pentecost was that God had exalted Jesus to his right hand. There is no doubt that the minds of those who were then converted were drawn towards this vision of the crucified and exalted Lord as their hearts were filled with the Holy Spirit (Acts 2:14–34). 'No one can say "Jesus is Lord"', said Paul, 'except by the Holy Spirit' (1 Cor 12:3).

'Where is the Lord, the God of Elijah?'

At the moment when Elijah '*ascended in a whirlwind into heaven*' (v.11), Elisha saw everything his leader had prayed to become the vision of his life-time. Suddenly another realm seemed to be opened before him. Here was One who ruled gloriously above and beyond all the earthly conflicts and challenges that he himself, now alone, was going to have to face in Israel. There came before his eyes, too, '*a chariot of fire and horses of fire*', a symbol of the enthusiasm and power that had brought strength and victory to Elijah in his earthly conflicts. He had taken the sight of them as a pledge that the same heavenly help would come to himself while he, too, continued the struggle. The cry of wonder and joy at the discovery was meant to be heard by the great man as he ascended. It was as if Elisha wanted his departing friend to know that it had really happened to him and that he was grateful. *'Father, Father!'* he exclaimed, 'I have seen all that you meant when you spoke to me!' He knew also from the moment he saw Elijah disappear that he was now going to be a changed man in thought, attitude and conviction, and he gave expression to his desire for it to happen by tearing his clothes in two as he picked up and put on the mantle which had fallen at his feet.

He now found himself emboldened to call to God for a spectacular sign. '*He took the mantle of Elijah that had fallen from him, and struck the water, saying, "Where is the LORD, the God of Elijah?" When he had struck the water, the water was parted to the one side and to the other, and Elisha went over*' (v.14).

We are here forced either seriously to question his action, or to marvel at it. He was no longer alone. There were fifty witnesses on the other side of the river of Jordan who saw and heard him. Had the miracle not happened he would have had no future as a prophet. Was he not putting God to the test and risking his whole career in doing so? When we think it over, however, and understand the circumstances, we tend rather to admire. He was giving full expression to the exultant confidence that had come to him with the vision. He also had the promise of Elijah that when that vision came, the power of the Spirit, in double portion, would be his too. '*If you see me as I am being taken from you, it will be granted you*' (v.10). The words of that promise were now ringing in his ears, and they seemed to be a solemn pledge from God himself that he was willing to be trusted on the spot to fulfil it. He not only had the promise of Elijah but also his personal example immediately before his mind. He himself had called on God for such a sign to enable him to cross the river.

The cry '*Where is the LORD, the God of Elijah?*' was a confession of liberating faith. Elijah's whole life stood before him now as a testimony to the reality and power of the God of Abraham, Isaac and Jacob, the God of Moses and of all his fathers to the faith. Now as Elijah's successor, he himself was giving his pledge that his father's God would be his too, that he would trust in the same redeeming love and draw his own strength from the same boundless, and never-failing source. The miracle of the dividing of the waters when it happened served, too, as a promise on the part of God that Elisha himself would never be put to shame when he called on the name of the Lord with faith and hope. Joshua himself, he would remember, had been given an identical word when he was left alone after the death of his great leader. 'As I was with Moses, so I will be with you: I will not fail you or forsake you. Be strong and courageous.' (Joshua 1:5–6)

We have no need today for such spectacular miraculous signs from God to assure us as we face our task in the world, nor do we have any call to seek them. But the Holy Spirit can give confidence and even boldness to those who are in themselves naturally timid and reserved. After Pentecost onlookers marvelled at the boldness of the early disciples. This boldness that is a gift of the Spirit is quite different from self-confidence. It is the boldness of one who trembles because one has no confidence in oneself. Our confidence comes because we have the Spirit of sonship in our hearts. We know indeed that we are the children of God and can cry boldly in prayer, 'Abba Father!' It is because we can make this prayer with such confidence that we can face the hard tasks of our life and service.

Our confidence like that of Elisha can also find inspiration in the example of those who have gone before us. The God we serve is the Lord God of our Fathers! Our circumstances, the kind of life we are meant to live, and the kind of world we have to live in, are all different from theirs, but the trials and difficulties we ourselves have to face are neither greater nor less than theirs were. We are meant to remember them, read about them and hold their example gratefully and hopefully before us.

Reality or Imagination?

The onlooking prophets who watched Elisha's return through the Jordan readily accepted the miraculous sign of power and authority now given to him by God. '*The spirit of Elijah rests on Elisha*' (v.15). When, however, he gave a realistic account of what he had 'seen', and what had happened to himself and Elijah at the moment of the whirlwind, Elisha found himself unable to convince them. They persisted in their suggestion that the vision could have been 'all in the mind'. They sent fifty men to search for three days either for the wandering prophet or his dead body. The curt brevity of Elisha's reply to their report of failure seems to reflect that even on their return, (after finding, as it were, the tomb empty!) they were inclined to scepticism. Yet the verse that introduces this whole chapter shows that at the time this Book of Kings was written, it was accepted as a fact of history that on a certain day the Lord took Elijah, '*up to heaven by a whirlwind*'.

Notes

A Unique Story — a Witness to Human Destiny?
This story has unique features that must affect our approach

to it, and that also prevent us from trying to make it the source of any ordinary lessons about life, or doctrines for theological edification. Its chief purpose is to pay tribute to one of the greatest figures in Old Testament history and in doing so it gives us a fugitive glimpse of the destiny God had planned especially for him. His achievement for God was outstanding. His departure from this earth must also be outstanding.

The fact that so much in the story is unexplained and symbolical fascinates us and challenges us to use our imagination to probe for an obviously intended meaning. Yet at the same time we are made to feel that here we are faced with a depth and mystery that continually remind us of the limits of our thought. We have the same difficulty with the story as the woman expected Jesus to have at the well: 'nothing to draw with, and the well is deep'! A notable feature of the story is that God is not mentioned, yet we are given the impression that every move and thought is being closely directed by him and that he is shaping the whole event.

We have suggested in our exposition that when this event was accepted as fact, the circulation of this story must have encouraged faith in a life after death. There is no doubt that it took centuries of experience under the grace of God for the people of Israel to rise to a strong and satisfying faith in what happens to a person after death. In this same book of Kings we will find that even Hezekiah on his death-bed feared that he was now 'consigned to the gates of Sheol' and would no longer 'see the Lord in the land of the living' (Isa. 38:11, cf. 2 Kings 20:1ff.) We have suggested in our exposition of 1 Kings that even David who momentarily in his Psalms could express a radiant hope in the life to come, could partly lose the vision on his own death-bed. We believe that this story should be taken into account when this subject is reviewed. Is it possible that the author of Psalm 73 was thinking of Elijah's ascension when he affirmed his personal belief that God would 'receive me with honor'?

The 'double share' of the Spirit
By law (Deut. 21:17) the first born son had the right to inherit

twice as much from his father as each of the other sons. Commentators suggest that Elisha had this law in mind, and was making the request not because he wanted to be a greater prophet than Elijah, but rather because he wanted to succeed as head of the community of prophets.

Points for Further Thought and Discussion

In Elijah's striking of the water a contrast is drawn between the frail old lonely man and what he was seeking to accomplish. Read e.g. Mat. 17:20, 1 Cor 1:27, 2 Cor 12:9. Do we, too often, allow our own natural human make-up and frailty to hold us back from progress in God's ways and success in God's work?

Following Elijah's stress on Elisha's need for vision, do we at times tend today so to stress our need for renewal and revival through the gifts and effects of the Holy Spirit to the neglect of our equally great need for a vision of what God has given us and done for us in Jesus? Should the latter have priority over the former?

In this whole incident both Elijah and Elisha seem to act without being given clear instructions. They obey intuitions that come to them on the spot, acting spontaneously on impulse. Compare e.g. the spontaneity of the woman who broke the box of precious ointment over Jesus, and his comments (Mark 14:3–9). Are we ourselves, sometimes or often, meant to act on such impulses (are there dangers here?), and do we leave enough room for such actions in the routine of our Church life?

Compare the account of the failure of Elisha to convince his followers about what had happened, with Luke 24:22–24 and John 20:24–25. What is it that we need besides our reports, to become convincing witnesses to Christ's resurrection? cf. Acts 1:8, John 20:18–20, Luke 24:31.

Elijah was at first tempted, in his natural desire to be alone, to withhold himself from those with whom God meant him to share his coming experience. Do we ourselves at times yield to the same temptation — and fail to be of full service to God?

CHAPTER III

ELISHA BECOMES INVOLVED
2 Kings 2:19–3:27

The Narrative

The men of Jericho believed that the well from which their community drew its water supply was polluted and was affecting the health and prosperity of their whole district, especially causing miscarriages. No doubt having heard news of what had taken place nearby among the sons of the prophets they accosted Elisha as he was passing through, and pled his help. With a word and sign Elisha healed the waters, thus bringing God's blessing to the area. Immediately after, however, passing through Bethel, faced by insult and contemptuous rejection he found himself forced to defend the sanctity of his new office by invoking a destructive attack by bears upon a gang of unruly youths. Shortly afterwards, entirely against his own will or desire he found himself involved in giving advice and help to the Kings of Israel and Judah and Edom in a critical military situation on an expedition to Moab. He responded in this case with much reluctance. His advice at first seemed to be brilliantly successful, but eventually the whole expedition had a disastrous and unprofitable end.

In Jericho

The leaders of the community at Jericho having heard, from the local prophets, some account of what had happened to Elisha at the Jordan, approached him as he passed through, with an account of their plight: '*The water is bad and the land is unfruitful*'. Some translations indicate that frequent miscarriages were taking place among the women and the cattle too. They found the condition all the more vexing because the site had great potential. Much thought, imagination and expense had been put into the fairly recent planning of the place, and they had had great hopes for its future.

Among possible explanations suggested today by commentators, one is that certain snails in the water were bearers of infection, another is that the waters of the spring had deep down contact with radio-active strata (see Wiseman, Comm. p. 197). Elisha probably did not imagine that the pollution could have had any such physical origin, but he was well aware of a psychological and spiritual anxiety that troubled many of the city's inhabitants. They remembered the curse that Joshua had placed on those who would dare to rebuild the city. It could be rebuilt only if the builder in doing so sacrificed both his firstborn and his youngest son (cf. Josh. 6:26). Hiel of Bethel was reputed to have made such a sacrifice when, in the early days of Ahab, he had laid the foundations of the new city (1 Kings 16:34). But what if Hiel had somehow only pretended to pay such a price or if in some way his heart in making the offering had not been right before God? There were stern and apt words in the book of Deuteronomy about the curses that could overtake 'city, ... field, ... the fruit of your womb, the fruit of the ground' if the people were not careful to observe God's commandments and his statutes (cf. Deut. 28:15–19). One commentator thinks that it was this 'superstition' in the mind alone that was behind all the trouble in the city.

Elisha's approach to the situation reveals his pastoral understanding of this haunting mental fear, and the need for complete assurance. Their first need was for a word from a prophet of God that could reverse the supposed spoken curse, and he uttered such a word with stark clarity: *'Thus says the Lord, "I have made this water wholesome; from now on neither death nor miscarriage shall come from it."'* In order to illustrate what his word was intended to do he also used the new vessel and the salt. These were meant not to produce, by their use, any unusual effect within the stream, but simply to represent the kind of result Elisha wanted to bring about through the word he had spoken. Commentators at various times have read varied meanings into the elements used. Some have dwelt on the fact that the bitterness of salt was a sign that the bitterness of human life can be cured only by bitter means, illustrating that it is only through the bitterness of Christ's Cross that we are given the real cure for our bitter human ways! D. J. Wiseman suggests that the new bowl may have been a symbol for purity, and that the salt could represent preservation 'pointing to cleansing ... and God's faithful covenant' (cf. 2 Chron. 13:5). Whatever ideas were in Elisha's mind as he used them he was acting as a pastor caring for the simple people around him, and trying to help them, to see and understand in a visible way the marvellous effect of the word he was about to speak in the name of the Lord.

In giving such priority to the spoken Word of God, Elisha was following the example of his former master. It was by the word and prayer that Elijah had brought God's will into effect within the life of Israel. It is true that Elisha as a pastor became at times more prone to use, and to make people use, visible signs and actions along with the word as he tried to meet the needs of the situation before him. But such signs and actions were meant only to be of service to the word. Jesus himself was a prophet 'mighty in deed and word' (Luke 24:19), but he, too, occasionally used signs to help people towards faith in his word (cf. John 9:6–7, 20:22). As he works today in our midst, he also uses water, bread and wine in Baptism and the Lord's Supper. These elements are in themselves very much the same as the cruse of salt — futile and insignificant things. Yet, used along with the word they can be a powerful means of cleansing and renewal within the life of the Church.

At Bethel

We can interpret Elisha's tragic experience at Bethel as being providential. After the doubts with which his own disciples had received his account of the ascension of Elijah, he needed the uplift and encouragement of his remarkable achievement at

Jericho. The news of it would eventually go round the local area and establish his reputation. Moreover it would serve within his own memory as a sign that God could use him again to do such things.

After such a spectacular reception and triumph, however, he needed now to be brought back to earth in order to learn that the life of a prophet in the service of God was going to involve him in bitter and perplexing conflict, and that he himself would sometimes fail to be at his best. It is helpful at this point to remember that immediately after the first sign at Cana of Galilee in which Jesus 'manifested his glory' he was then led to go to Jerusalem where he had his first experience of the vicious opposition that was to lead him to his Cross.

'*Some small boys*' says our present account, '*came out of the city and jeered at him, saying "Go away, baldhead. Go away baldhead!"*' Recent translators soften our dislike for what was about to happen by pointing out that the word used in the text enables us to regard those who encountered Elisha as grown, responsible, 'youths'. It is also pointed out in Elisha's defence that their words did not convey merely a personal insult to Elisha on account of his physical appearance but reflected the hardened local contempt for the prophets of the Lord bred in them by their parents. The town of Bethel had become the centre of a community opposed to the covenant religion of the Lord upheld by Elijah and Elisha. These youths were well versed in songs that mocked this old tradition and they may have been organised to meet him and to sing them as a warning that he was not wanted in this area.

We naturally feel some shock, however, at what happened, and at Elisha's part in the incident. Before we make a final judgment there are several important considerations to hold before our minds. We need not suppose that either the writer who deliberately included the story in his history, or Elisha himself had any pride in what happened, or were telling the story for our entire approval. Indeed we need not imagine that Elisha himself later remembered this incident with anything but shame for his own part in it. He had to learn by experience that in the tasks he sometimes had to do for God, he could himself make serious blunders. He changed as he became more mature. Later on we will discover that he shrank almost with horror as he had to utter the word of judgment that he knew would inevitably bring widespread human suffering to the people of Israel. It is not necessary for us to conclude that God himself approved of Elisha's conduct even while he supported him. God hates his name to be publicly degraded and his name to be verbally blasphemed, and the critical situations where an over zealous prophet invokes his protection and vindication (as in the case of Elijah versus Ahaziah see pp. 6–7) he at times has to side with his prophet.

It is important that we do not become so absorbed in the moral intricacies of this perplexing incident to miss the chief lessons that our narrator is trying to bring out here. The same ministry of grace which brought healing to Jericho, had the opposite effect in Bethel when it was rejected and mocked. The New Testament constantly reminds us that when God offers us his grace and mercy today we too are free either to accept or reject, either to honour or insult, and it adds repeated warnings. Paul, describing the effect of his preaching, says that to the one it is 'a fragrance from death to death, to the other a fragrance from life to life' (2 Cor. 2:16). Speaking of any community that would not receive him, by rejecting his disciples, Jesus said 'It will be more tolerable on the day of judgment for the land of Sodom and Gomorrah than for that town' (Matt. 10:15).

We are, no doubt, meant to notice, too, a further aspect of the contrast brought out in these two happenings. Jericho was a city which, years before, had come under a curse. Bethel was a place God had visited with blessing. Now under Elisha things are reversed. Jericho is blessed, Bethel is cursed. Let us never imagine, the story says to us, that the grace of God ever clings to a place or a race, or that a curse can be transmitted automatically from one generation to another. What matters is the decision that men and women make about the Word of God that confronts them here and now.

In the Campaign Against Moab

It is characteristic of Elisha's career that at first especially he shrank from political involvement, confining himself mostly to a pastoral ministry amongst the needy and anxious. A war, however, broke out. Mesha the King of Moab had not only refused to pay his annual tribute to the King of Israel, but was harassing Israelite ex-patriates who lived there, and was threatening important trade routes. Jehoram the King of Israel had persuaded the Kings of Judah and Edom to join in an expedition to crush him.

When the war began Elisha did not seek nor receive any word from God that might involve him in a public ministry and he made no attempt to meet or contact the king. But he felt it his responsibility to be there in the expedition, as an unofficial chaplain along with the troops. It was suddenly and very reluctantly that he found himself the central figure in an important international war cabinet meeting. The expedition had come to the point of disaster. Facing the main Moabite defences the kings found themselves entirely without any water for horses or men and were at their wits' end. So desperate were they that when a junior officer mentioned that a young prophet, a friend of Elijah, who had begun to show himself gifted, was there on the field, he was sought out and brought in to the consultation.

Several considerations will help us to understand the exchange of words that took place when Elisha was introduced to his king. The young prophet shared Elijah's attitude to the royal house of Omri and at this stage in his career he was no doubt apt to imitate even in manner the bluntness of his great predecessor. Even though Jehoram could piously use the name of 'the Lord' he suspected that he merely shared the hypocrisy of his grandfather Ahab. His rudeness to the king was due not to bad temper or natural disposition but to his hatred of Baalism and of any superficial service of the truth.

We can easily understand his hesitancy in responding to the sudden demand for a word from the Lord. He had already had no pre-intimation that he was going to be called upon to give divine guidance. He had been taken aback by the sudden intrusion on his privacy. Possibly he himself had not approved of this expedition in the first place. After all, it was an aggressive campaign, and he may have had a premonition that it was going to end up in disaster. What could he say? We can understand, therefore, why under those circumstances he called for 'a musician'. Though music had been sometimes associated with inspiration in the prophetic circles in which he moved (cf. 1 Sam. 10:5, 16:16) we need not conclude that in his own present case he believed that the music could put him in touch with God. He wanted it, rather, simply to give him time to overcome his reluctance to be involved, to pray and to open his mind towards God.

It must have been a relief to him that he was not involved in doing any more than simply to make the announcement that the next day the whole military situation would be marvellously reversed. The water would be there for them in floods. The Moabites in the strongholds would be deluded to attack them by mistaking the water for blood. They would come to the scene off their guard and if the three Kings were alert they would have the enemy and their fortress in their hands.

The 'miracle' which is here attributed to Elisha is best understood if we regard it as a miracle of foresight arising from a uniquely given understanding of the atmospheric conditions of the day. It is often explained that a sudden and distant great thunderstorm in the mountains was taking place causing great floods of water to move in the direction of the beleaguered army.

Elisha's insight and advice certainly saved the momentary situation. Yet we soon discover that his intervention here at this stage in his career had no notable impact on the destiny of the people of God and brought nobody any good. The King of Moab in the battle grew more and more desperate in his resistance and the battle became more and more fierce. Finally in a last effort at salvation he '*took his first-born son who was to succeed him and offered him as a burnt offering on the wall. And great wrath came upon Israel; so they withdrew from him and returned to their own land*' (3:27). What does this mean? It has been suggested that King Mesha offered his son as a sacrifice to his god Chemosh because a plague had broken out in the city, and that the allied armies fled for fear that the contagion would spread to themselves. It seems more likely that the allies being superstitious were themselves sickened and horrified at the thought of such a sacrifice being made, and fled out of fear of its result.

Whatever caused the retreat no one came back from that expedition with any credit. Certainly not Elisha! He himself must have been shocked not only at the ignominious finale but at the wanton destruction of the trees and the stopping up of the wells (3:25). It was a healthy warning to him that to become involved in war and politics could lead a 'man of God' into much dubious, pointless and sometimes harmful activity. This early experience reinforced the lesson he had partly been taught at Bethel. We find him for the remaining early years of his ministry concentrating on pastoral work and avoiding the political arena till he found himself gradually and almost unwittingly again involved.

Note

The Elisha Stories (1) — The Biographical Element
There is a tendency among commentators to regard the stories about Elisha as mainly a collection of legendary tales treasured here and there in the memory of various companies of prophets, often arising out of local incidents and emphasising his power to work miracles. The writer of Kings, it is believed, has simply strung these loosely together without much regard for chronological order. We ourselves have preferred to understand them as forming a consistent biography of the prophet. Taking them in this way we believe we have been given important clues as to how the writer meant them to be understood.

Elisha, we believe, knew from the beginning of his career the important and decisive part that he was destined to play in the political affairs of his country. He knew that he had, however, to wait a considerable time for the situation to develop, and first of all he had to win the confidence and respect of those whose co-operation he would require in the action that would then have to be taken.

We have suggested that from the beginning of his ministry he shrank by nature from the brutal and compromising involvement in such military and international affairs, and the human suffering he would cause by obedience to this aspect of his calling (cf. 1 Kings 19:17) and we have suggested that a clue to his behaviour and attitude during the long waiting period is to be found in his desire to express his witness in more pastoral ways, revealing rather God's intimate care for individuals around him in their daily needs. In this he differed from Elijah who was forced to assume political leadership. (Though Elijah's achievement and deserved reputation in the service of God rank him alongside Moses in greatness, we have already noted his short-coming in pastoral understanding!)

We have therefore interpreted the stories about Elisha as arranged to bring out this aspect of his development as a prophet. We try to show how gradually in a providential way, his reputation abroad and his status within his own community put him in the position finally to do the task for which Elijah had anointed him. It is noteworthy that even at this final high point in his career he again reveals a reluctance to enter any close alliance with unstable and self-willed political leaders.

Points for Further Thought and Discussion

In creating the world and in bringing his power to bear upon the human situation God is described often as using simply a 'word' or words. (Gen. 1:3; Ps. 33:6, 9; Ezek. 37:1–6). Jesus in doing miracles often confined himself to the use of simply a word. Yet occasionally, as we have seen, God encouraged also the use of signs and objects by those engaged in his work, and Jesus in the sacraments ordained the use of bread, wine and water. It has often been suggested that God gives us these signs and sacraments, appealing to more senses than that of hearing, because being creatures of sense, we need more than a mere word to bring us to full conviction. He thus, therefore, caters for our need. A Scottish preacher once insisted that the sacraments give us no more than the word by itself would give us, but they do help to give us a 'better grip' of Christ. Is this apt? Are we depriving ourselves if we do not use the sacraments regularly? Is it correct to think of the sacraments as bringing us no more than the word does?

Preachers have sometimes used this picture of the plight of Jericho to illustrate the situation that prevails in many modern communities where so much that is good and pleasant becomes utterly spoiled by an evil that seems to come from the human heart (cf. Matt. 15:19) and that can be cured only by Christ. A poet once wrote: 'where every prospect pleases, and only man is vile'. Is this comparison valid, and apt?

Can you understand, and give reasons for Elisha's reluctance at this time of his life, to be involved in power politics? Do such reasons apply to us within the Church today and is such reluctance justifiable? Was Elisha's bluntness with Jehoram justifiable?

What is music for? Calvin suggested from Gen. 4:21, that it was a gift of God given in the mercy of God, to sinful men in their alienation from God, to help to make this hard life tolerable and pleasant ('Art thou weary? Music shall charm thee!'). Is there any suggestion in Holy Scripture that the inspiration of music can by itself put us in touch with God, and enable us to receive the Holy Spirit? What place should music have within the Church?

These incidents show that even though God was very close to Elisha, and using him for his purposes, he was not continuously successful or faithful. He found himself falling short, and experienced failure. Are we meant to take encouragement as well as warning from this trend in these stories?

CHAPTER IV

ELISHA —ON HOME GROUND
2 Kings 4:1–37

The Narrative

The two stories in this section are from accounts of Elisha's early pastoral activity. In the first, the prophet is appealed to by the widow of a former prophet whose sons were threatened with enslavement because of her debts. He meets her need by setting the stage in her house for the miraculous multiplication of oil. What happens in the second story takes place in the home of a wealthy woman who gives hospitality to the prophet. Since she is childless the prophet decides to bestow on her the miraculous gift of a son, who after a few years of life suddenly dies. Much of the story is taken up by a fascinating and profound account of how the child is finally restored to life.

Elisha — the Pastor

It is worthwhile noting some of the features of the public image we are given of Elisha as we read these chapters before us. Quite unlike Elijah he is easily located and always readily available. He becomes, in the word of the little serving maid in Syria, 'the prophet who is in Samaria' (5:3), where he has a house — perhaps a clinic! He seems to move around in a regular routine. He can be easily waylaid by people who have needs and is ready to be interrupted. He is anxious to hear about people's wants, and to be asked how he can help. People are attracted to him. He seems to be popular and yet, though friendly he never descends to any kind of cheap familiarity.

He is a 'man of God' set apart and separate, held in profound respect, indeed with some awe.

The disillusionment that came to Elisha through the Moabite fiasco, seems to have led him to concentrate for a considerable time on what we ourselves might tend to regard as rather obscure and unimportant pastoral work described in the next two chapters which are now before us. His pastoral instincts were stronger than his political instincts, and he was more at home with ordinary people than in the courts and councils of the land. We will find him always deeply attracted to the fellowship of the prophetic communities.

In following this instinct and this course he believed he was not in any way shirking his duty as the successor of Elijah or withdrawing from involvement in the decision-making that controls history and directs human affairs. He understood the supreme importance of what was happening when the word and will of God was brought to bear upon the private domestic lives of those who then did not even have a vote, and were more often than not the victims of the politics pursued by others. He believed that such pastoral activity could further the Kingdom of God in the life of Israel. The author of the Book of Kings also understood this too. This is why he was careful to include in his account of Elisha's life so many of these pastoral incidents. To him, these had to be given a worthy place of notice among the events by which God was moving the history of Israel in the way he wanted it to go.

This insight into the supreme importance in our human life of the personal and pastoral aspects of the service of God was, of course, emphasised by Jesus himself. A prominent aspect of his teaching was that the Word of God, sown within the individual human heart through pastoral and preaching activity within Church and home, wherever it was cordially received, was bound inevitably to have an irresistible influence in bringing about the Kingdom of God through its remarkable hidden power of growth (cf. Matt. 13:4–9, Mk. 4:26–29). Jesus, in his ministry on earth, found the pattern of the work he was meant to do described for him in various parts of Old Testament scripture. He had in his mind, for example, the pictures of the Suffering Servant of God given in the book of Isaiah. In the Sermon on the Mount he cast himself in the role of a new Moses giving a new law to his disciples. He also as he went about his ministry seems to have had in mind the example of this humble prophet (see note on pp. 60 and 54) going about among ordinary people, helping them, healing and especially speaking a word directed personally to the need their individual case presented. We take note at this point, that like Elisha, Jesus greatly valued an entrance into people's homes (cf. John 2:1-11, Luke 19:1- 5).

With the Widow — a Sign from God

The story has much more to tell us than the mere fact that such a remarkable miracle of the multiplication of oil was one of the kind deeds done by Elisha for the poor. When Israel began to displace the Lord by turning to other gods their social system itself ceased to reflect his justice and mercy. The God of Israel cared especially for the widows and fatherless. He had given his sanction to many laws that protected them from falling into irredeemable debt and their children from being sold into slavery. Through disregard for law, and the introduction of Baalism, however, people had grown heedless and the weak were now being dispossessed by the strong and ruthless. Naboth, for instance, had been robbed of his land and cruelly murdered by the local authorities at Jezreel under the influence of Baalism.

The woman in this case is presented to us here as the victim of such social change. Finding herself hopelessly in debt and her sons being enslaved she understood well what was taking place around her. Her heart was crying out not simply for personal help, but for justice, and for God to vindicate her right. She seemed drawn to Elisha on this account. Surely the prophet of God will listen to the cry of the oppressed, and if he is a man of God he will seek to put things right! What Elisha immediately did is to be interpreted as a sign that God himself cared, that he was a witness to such wrong-doing among his people, and was prepared to execute justice for the fatherless and widow.

If we are fully to appreciate what he did we must understand that it was not the task then allotted to him by God to call publicly for widespread social reform. This was to be work of the two great preaching prophets, Amos and Hosea, whom God would, a generation or two later, raise up in Israel for this purpose. Baalism had first of all to be destroyed before such social action was possible. The role to which Elisha in his day was especially called was to strike first of all at the roots of this false religion and we will see that he did not hesitate to do this when his call to public action came to him. In the circumstances before him he did what he was marvellously fitted and able to do. He gave his witness to God's mercy and justice not in words, but in an act of practical help and compassion. It was a sign that God heeded the cry of those who were calling on him to 'execute justice for the fatherless and widow' (Deut. 10:18; Ps. 68:5).

With the Widow — 'Pay your debts and live!'

Approaching the details of this story it is helpful to remember the different ways which Jesus took, and the varied means he used, when he healed and helped people. Sometimes like Elijah he spoke a bare word (Mk. 4:39). Sometimes the accomplishment of the miracle demanded obedient action on the part of those involved (Lk. 17:14, Mk. 3:5, Mt. 17:27). Here it is a case of having to take step after step simply in obedience to a word given to her with no explanation of the end from the beginning. She has to believe where she does not see, and to go on when she does not understand.

Though he used marvellously the obedience his word inspired, we must not, however, fail to notice how, as he enlisted her obedience, he also elicited from her a confession of her personal sense of utter helplessness. It comes out beautifully in the New English Bible translation. 'Tell *me what you have in the house*', he asked her, '*Nothing at all*', *she answered*, '*except a flask of oil*' (v. 2). The way she put it is significant. So overwhelming is the debt that is facing her that she can do 'Nothing' towards meeting it. The '*flask of oil*' is a mere afterthought. It is part of the '*nothing at all*'.

It is worth while at this point turning our thought to the teaching of the New Testament where we hear this emphatic 'nothing' echoed to us time and again. We hear it most powerfully when we look at the Cross — 'Nothing in my hand I bring' — nothing that can now even be mentioned alongside what it has cost him to bring us our salvation! It comes home to us day by day as we live our lives in him — as having nothing, and yet possessing everything (2 Cor 6:10). As we receive what comes to us from him, always we find ourselves empty, always only receivers! It is brought home to us in Jesus' reminder that, with all the dedication, skill and fervour we put into our efforts in his service, unless he himself is there, the giver of the opportunity, and the inspiration in carrying it through — it is all nothing! (John 15:5).

One aspect of her obedience was her willingness to depend on her neighbours. It is a pleasant relief to read of those neighbours, and to realise that in those days the world was peopled not only by creditors and thieves but also by ordinary folk who were willing to act with kindness. We, too, in our own need, no matter how harshly this world has used us, must remember that sometimes God is seeking to help us through our neighbours, as he is seeking to help our neighbours through us. We can therefore thank him that he sometimes surrounds us with people by whom he brings help and kindness into our lives. The apostle Paul, after his conversion, passed through a time of confusion and perplexity. God did not help him directly from heaven with another spectacular vision. Instead, God blessed him through Ananias, a man near at hand (Acts 9:10–17). It is a tragedy to see Christians too proud or nervous to seek or accept help that can come to them in their need from fellow Christians. Even Jesus was not too proud to accept comfort and encouragement from friends. He often went to the house of Martha and Mary, and of Lazarus, where his human heart was refreshed. He must have felt that such friendship at that time was a gift from his Father.

Moreover, she had to '*shut the door*' upon herself and upon her sons who brought the jars to her. The neighbours did not see the wonderful use God made of the pots they lent to this widow. They never realised how gloriously God used the acts of kindness he challenged them to do to this poor woman. It is often so in life. As long as we live on this earth we may never know to what use God has put our cup of cold water, our cheerful greeting, our kind word, our helping hand, our little gift. In the great scene at the Judgment Throne in the parable of the sheep and the goats, (Matthew 25:31–46), Jesus pictured himself as saying to those who entered his glory, 'Come, you that are blessed by my Father ... for I was hungry and you gave me food.' 'Lord, when was it that we saw you hungry?' they said in surprise. The deeds God most uses to bring blessing to others may be the deeds we do almost unconsciously because we think they are insignificant. We hardly know we are doing them. Yet behind the scenes, behind the shut doors, God is working through them his miracles of grace and power.

Is it not true also today that important events in the life we live for God can happen 'behind shut doors' as it is here? They may happen sometimes in answer to prayer, sometimes quite unexpectedly. They may be quite private affairs which no one else might fully understand. Yet we see with our own eyes they are miraculous signs of God's love and power (cf. Ps. 118:23).

We are meant to notice, also that she herself could have had more if she had borrowed more vessels (v. 6). There was no limit to what he wanted to do for her. How near we are here again to the New Testament in the thoughts that inevitably come to us! Having paid such a great price to set us free, does he not want freely also to 'give us everything else' (Rom. 8:32)? How much more might we have from him if we ceased limiting him and opened our lives and homes up more to the great things he has prepared for those who take him fully at his word!

With the Shunammite — the Crisis

The prophet Elijah, early in his career, found himself in a critical situation when he was challenged by the widow at Zarephath to raise her son from the dead. Here Elisha finds himself faced also by a woman with a like challenge. The similarities in the two stories are, however, very superficial. God does not repeat himself. There are very great differences in how the crisis in each case occurs, and the nature of the test of each incident arises as much out of these differences as out of the similarities.

We have to allow ourselves to be led towards the account of this crisis in our present story by following the fascinating details of the narrative. Skinner points out that the picture it brings before us 'is of great interest for the light it throws on many details of the social life in ancient Israel'. We shall find it of even more interest for what it tells us about the character and attitude of the woman who invited Elisha into her house. Most of the recent translations describe her as a 'rich' woman. She certainly had material wealth but she was also rich in the godly influence which she could shed around her (the A.V. calls her a 'great' woman!). Her charity was expressed in feeding the hungry, and this practice brought her into contact with Elisha, who often passed by her house. He always seemed hungry enough and was never too proud to accept her help. Her care and concern for him as a '*holy man of God*' led to her suggestion to her husband that they make a '*chamber*' in their roof, fully furnished to suit his needs as an overnight place to stay when he was on his rounds.

Time passed, and finally Elisha wanted to express his gratitude. Could he do something for her in return? By this time he had come to know people at the court and in the upper ranks of the army. Could he use his influence there in any way to bring her favour? He seemed to go at this point to the verge of patronising and offending her, and her dignified answer should have warned him against going any further along this line: '*I dwell among my own people.*' These words give us a glimpse of her inner strength and peace of heart. They are an expression of serene contentment with God and all the gifts he has already showered upon her. How could a prophet of God expect her to covet any more than his grace had already given her?

It was at Gehazi's prompting however that Elisha (he must have been inspired by God to do so!) uttered the disturbing and fateful word promising a child. Her reply to the suggestion that this should happen is as self-revealing as was her reply to the offer of social advancement. '*No, my lord, O man of God: do not deceive your servant.*' Like all the childless women of her age she had had to face all the trials that her condition involved — the anxieties, the frequently frustrated hopes, the false accusations from ignorant neighbours and friends (perhaps even from her husband!), and the temptation to feel bitterness before God. It had no doubt been a long drawn out struggle involving deep self-questioning, and we can imagine that her faith had almost gone. But she had won the battle, denied her self-will, overcome all her alien doubts about God's goodness and re-oriented her life entirely to his service and glory — and now, here was this thoughtless man (and he a man of God!) seeking to open up the wound that long ago had been healed by self-sacrifice and the love of God!

Yet, in spite of her first shocked protest, the word Elisha spoke began to take root in her mind and she became pregnant. She began to rejoice, as Sarah had learned to do, that nothing was 'too wonderful for the Lord' (Gen. 18:14). The child became a token to her that the faith which accepts God's word with pure simplicity will never be ashamed. She took pride in telling the story of how God gave him to her by miracle and the word of the prophet.

Everything suddenly changed. *'When the child was older, he went out one day to his father among the reapers. He complained to his father, "Oh my head, my head"! The father said to his servant, "Carry him to his mother"; he carried him, and brought him to his mother; the child sat on her lap till noon, and he died* (vv. 19—20).

With the Shunammite — the Questioning and the Agony

When death takes away our dear ones, even our children, we have to learn ultimately to resign. When their house fell on Job's young people and killed them, he pleased God when he managed to say 'The Lord gave and the Lord has taken away; blessed be the name of the Lord' (Job 1:21). Yet our Christian faith also at the same time must refuse to accept what death does to us. God did not design life so that bereavement such as this was meant to happen, and we are not meant to accept the thought that it can ultimately be allowed to break up a dear relationship that has been richly blessed by Christ.

Though the circumstances of the birth of her child left this woman in quite a unique position, we ourselves can at least admire her and even learn something important to ourselves from the way her faith argued with God and his prophet. She rebelled at what had happened. She said to herself that this could not be God's will. Indeed it must be the Devil's will! God had promised her a child, and he had not meant to mock her through that promise. She refused to believe that this could be the end of the blessing that God had brought into her life when he gave her this child. After all, she had not even asked God for this child. He had come to her as a gift spontaneously offered by him out of his goodness. The Lord who had been responsible for bringing this sunshine into her life would make himself responsible for seeing that it was kept there.

Therefore she acted throughout as if this particular death was a short and accidental interlude in a story in which everything must turn out well. '*It will be all right,*' she said to her husband. She refused to say much more to anyone. To discuss it with others who did not understand what faith meant might have discouraged her. They might have spoken of accepting the situation. They might have spoken of funeral arrangements. '*It will be all right,*' she said to everyone, and she called for her ass and her servant and went to the prophet of God. Even with Gehazi, who was sent by Elisha to meet her, she refused to discuss the matter. She did not relax or rest until she was able to pour out her wild and desperate feelings to Elisha himself. She told him the whole story. She let him know that this matter was his responsibility, and she did not intend to let go of him until it was put right. '*Did I ask my lord for a son?*' she cried. '*Did I not say, Do not mislead me?*'

It was a strong argument. 'You,' she said to God's representative, 'you and your God interfered with my life in order to please me. I never asked nor sought this blessing. You forced it upon me, and I accepted it in good faith. I let my heart love this little one, for you encouraged me to expect that I had a right to the happiness he brought. He was a freely given reward for what I did in God's name. Now that he has been taken from me, I look to you to accept your responsibility to restore him.' '*As the Lord lives, and as you yourself live, I will not leave without you.*'

Such was the kind of faith that allowed God to fulfil his word perfectly to this woman of Shunem. It was a faith that sought to lay hold and to keep hold, not only of the promises, but of the promiser. It was a faith that endured in the face of delay, and battled for the fulfilment of the word against all contradiction. It was a faith that refused to accept from God only half a blessing but insisted on the full blessing. If this woman had accepted only the half blessing, and had buried her child, she would after all have received some benefit from the word of God. Her reproach would have been removed. She would have had a few years of happiness to look back upon and some blessed memories to cheer her. She could have spoken to others of how God had once in a miraculous way answered her prayers and fulfilled her desires. After all, to receive all that from the word of God would have been much better than to receive nothing! But she refused to allow God to stop halfway, and insisted on his going the whole way he had promised.

Though Elisha recognised the '*bitter distress*' the woman was in, his immediate response was strangely out of character. He seems at this time in his ministry to have lapsed into a superficiality, out of touch both with God and with what life was really doing to people around him — as if sending Gehazi to perform a correct ceremony with his staff on the face of the child (a little touch of magic!) could possibly meet the situation, or bring even a moment's assurance to the desperate mother! The woman herself realized the futility of the cheap attempt before Gehazi even started out, and therefore protestingly clung to the presence of the prophet, probably compelling him to follow his servant and pestering him to listen and take better heed. Eventually she let him go up to the little room alone, with all her accusations on his mind, and shut the door.

His self questioning must have begun at some point on his journey. Did she really have good grounds for her accusation that he was a deceiver? Had he himself really been under the inspiration of God when he had uttered the promise that she would have a child? Might he have lost touch with God? They were questions that put at stake his whole ministry. If he could not cope with this situation before him, how could he ever cope with the troubles of Israel?

When he had shut the door, the pitiful sight of the dead child before him must have intensified his sense of guilt, his anxiety and shame over his failure and his grief for the mother. He no longer had the serene confidence in asking with which he had formerly prayed for her to become pregnant. He realised how foolish had been his trust in the kind of routine and ritual he had taught Gehazi to use. Instead of laying his staff on the face of the child he laid himself over the little one as far as he possibly could, to identify himself with the death and misery that now faced him, pouring himself out in repentant self-sacrifice to God. He breathed on the child as if he wanted some of his own life to be imparted to heal the situation.

The prayer was answered, and the whole experience was, providentially, important in his development as a prophet. His great last experience with Elijah beyond the Jordan had brought home to him his continual need for vision and power from above; now he is learning about intercession, and its place in a prophet's life. How faithfully God seeks to hold on to those he calls to be his helpers in the Church, even though at times we so easily lapse! How carefully he plans our training and our way, and equips us for the work we have to do!

Notes

The Elisha Stories (2) — The Miraculous Element
God continually exercises a providential control over and within the history of all nations. It is, however, within the history of Israel that we find him specially active and more closely at work with the purpose of bringing about the salvation of the world in Christ. The history of Israel is indeed sometimes marked off from the rest of history by being called a 'salvation history'. God is interpreted as exercising a unique control over its direction through his word. 'This history', says Von Rad, 'is kept in motion and is guided to its God-oriented goal by the constantly intruding divine word' (cf. Is. 55:10–11 and the example already given in note on p. 12).

The immediate effects of this constantly impinging Word on the history and people of Israel are often obscure. At times no spectacular signs mark the fact that God is in Israel's midst, moving and controlling this people towards their unique destiny. Yet he is there shaping their history, faith and character within the ordinary routine of their national and family life, forgiving and training them to pray and continually answering their prayers, sustaining and supporting them when things are difficult, bringing them surely through grief and trouble, giving them enough light on the darkest problems of human life so that without receiving all the answers they seek, they come closer to him in their struggles. All that God accomplishes in this long drawn out and hidden process over centuries in the realm of thought, the formation of human character and truly oriented devotion to himself is miraculous. As Wheeler Robinson once said, 'The supreme miracle of the Old Testament is the historical development of the religion of Israel' (see for much of the following our note in 'Readings in 1 Kings' pp. 115–117).

There are, however, times within this salvation history when the opposition to the gradual realisation of God's word and will becomes especially intractable, and God has to act, as Jacques Ellul puts it, in 'a surprising and disruptive fashion'. He 'shatters the course of the natural' and forces man to confront himself and his will. Signs are clearly given that here within this history his word is powerfully at work, and events become 'transparent with miracle'. The possibility for such things to happen is there in the background of the whole historical development. Calvin notes at one point in his commentary on the Psalms that there is mention of God's 'wondrous deeds' — 'these signal and memorable benefits' — he calls them,'in which God has exhibited a bright and shining manifestation of divine power'. 'God,' he says, 'is the author of *all* blessings, but some have specially evident marks' (on Psalm 9:1). Though all God's works, as viewed in the Old Testament perspective, are wonderful, yet at particular points of time and space (to cite Wheeler Robinson again) 'the wonder of what is happening is intensified'. 'A miracle,' says Dibelius, 'is an event in which the hand of God, which is always there, can be more clearly traced than at other times.' Miracles dramatically reveal an activity which is continually taking place.

When we regard miracles in this light it is notable that God is so sparing in his uses of them in the Old Testament. They occur mostly in clusters at two critical periods in the history — during the period of the Exodus and wilderness wanderings, and during the period when Israel's faith was under its most serious threat from falsehood and Baalism. Calvin notes that the extraordinary miracles of God happen where and when there is a special need for them. Discussing the miracle of the rod turned into a serpent he underlines the fact that Moses, outwardly unimpressive and weak (an earthen vessel) had to be 'rendered formidable' to Pharaoh by God (Comm. on Exod. 7:10). The miracles authenticate the witness of the prophets. Moreover, through them God not only demonstrates his presence and power but also illuminates his purpose and the nature of his will and message. As one commentator puts it 'God used miracle to teach us truths about himself, his nature and purposes, which he could express in no other way.'

On Elisha's Care of the Widow

We believe that the teaching of the Old Testament justifies us in interpreting Elisha's response to the widow's need primarily as a sign of his prophetic social concern. Priority of place is always given to widows and orphans as a class when there is any call for deliverance of the oppressed, for it is recognised that they are among the first to suffer when society loses its sense of God. (Cf. Isa. 10:2, Jer. 7:1.) One of the names by which God willed himself to be called was 'Father of orphans, and protector of widows' (Ps. 68:5) and it is to be characterisic of his people that their welfare should always have priority in social action (Ex. 22:21–4, Zech. 7:10). It is the essential qualification of a man of God that he should be their counsellor and helper (Job 29:12, 31:16–17).

On Elisha's Symbolic Prayer-gesture

We believe that when Jesus went to Nain (the town that was originally Shunem) with the purpose of raising the widow's son, he had it deliberately in mind to do a miracle corresponding to that of Elisha there (see p. 60) It may be significant that as well as raising him by prayer and the word, he also in this case quite deliberately and dramatically touched the bier. Commentators have sometimes regarded this as a physical sign that he himself was on his way to identfying himself with our state of death, and taking upon himself its curse so that in its place and in exchange he could communicate to us his own resurrection life. Are we correct in thinking that Elisha, when he lay face to face, hand to hand over the child, and tried to breathe life into him, had in his mind the idea of making such an exchange? Some of the Church fathers saw in this action the foreshadowing of the 'wondrous exchange' Christ made with our humanity through his incarnation and death and resurrection.

Points for Further Thought and Discussion

Think of the marvellous use God made of the willingness of these neighbours to lend each a few empty pots. They did not know what he was going to do with them when they were asked. Read Mat. 10:42, 25:37–38. Why are we sometimes not ready to respond in little matters like this? Might Jesus' warning to 'be ready' (Mat. 24:44; Luke 12:35) apply in this case?

This woman of Shunem is an example of a rich person who was wholly devoted to God. So, of course, was Abraham. What did Jesus mean when he spoke of the extreme difficulty of the rich entering heaven? (Luke 18:25).

Compare the persistence of this Shunammite towards Elisha in her rebellious faith, with the persistent refusal of the woman from Tyre to be put off when Jesus and his disciples at first did so much to turn her away (cf. Mat. 15:21–28). What lessons does this added example reinforce?

Think of ways in which we ourselves can lapse into the same kind of superficiality as seemed at this time to affect Elisha. What might be the reasons behind such a development? Is it widespread?

There are many passages in Scripture which remind us of the lesson learned by Elisha, i.e. that there cannot be fruitfulness in Church work without travail (cf. Isa. 66:8) or tears (cf. Acts 20:31). Note that Jesus raised Lazarus after agonizing prayer (Jn. 11:33–35, 41). How can we secure a worthy place for such intercession within the Church today?

Why do you think the woman avoided letting her husband know anything about what had happened or where she was going?

CHAPTER V

THREE EARLY MIRACLES
2 Kings 4:38–44, 6:1–7

The Narrative

Of these stories about the early ministry of Elisha among the companies of the prophets, the first is of how he was able to counteract the effect of a poisonous herb which had been mistakenly thrown into a large pot of stew. The second is of how he presided at a meal during which a large company were satisfyingly fed from a wholly inadequate but well intentioned provision of food. The third is of how a poor prophet's axehead which had fallen into a river was miraculously recovered.

Elisha and the 'Company of Prophets'

In Elisha's day in various places, companies of prophets, all with a similar purpose and aim, were to be found here and there in Israel. These groups had their origin in earlier charismatic bands of religious people drawn together by a common desire to serve God within their community, given at times to ecstatic experience under, they believed, the influence of the Spirit of the Lord. By Elisha's time they became larger and more locally settled. The miracle of the widow's oil shows us that wives and families could belong to them, and suggests that they were communities without any guaranteed source of income and little wealth. They seem to have believed that since God had called them so fully to devote themselves to his service, they could trust him to provide for them. They expected that the bare needs of life that were not met by community effort would be supplied by the generosity of others prompted to share with them what they could give.

We can recognise the strain of Old Testament piety that is reflected in the adoption of such a way of life. We are reminded, for example, of the fifth verse of Psalm 37:

'Commit your way to the Lord
    trust in him, and he will act,

and of the experience spoken of in v. 25:

I have been young, and now am old,
yet I have not seen the righteous forsaken
or their children begging bread.'

Of course such followers of this way knew also that, at times, experience under God could seem to be contradictory. They could find themselves living on the verge of tragedy and want, finding that the wicked rather than the righteous seemed to prosper (cf. Ps. 73:1-3). Yet the mysteries of God's providence did not cancel out the certainties, and when they were in deep perplexity their faith could hold, and where others despaired, they believed God could work all things together for good.

We can admire Elisha's willingness to become closely associated with such communities. We find them at times treated with disdain by people close to government (cf. 2 Kings 9:11) and they were not in the favour of the religious establishment in temple or priestly circles. Though the great Elijah in his old age seems to have turned to them for fellowship for a short period, a leading prophet like Amos, could, later, publicly dissociate himself from them (Amos 7:14). Obviously the compiler of this account of Elisha's life believed that Elisha's sympathy with these groups was worthy of note, and that his activity among them should be given a prominent place alongside his other pastoral and political achievements in his account of the man. It was to the prophet's credit that he recognised that such people were being used by God, and, that he cared about the welfare of their widows and orphans. He obviously believed that the stories of the miracles which marked Elisha's association with them were genuine, and were signs of God's approval of his ministry among them.

God's Grace at the 'Lower Levels of Life'

Readers of the Old Testament who are sceptical about its occasional stories of miraculous happenings are apt to dismiss especially this section of the historical narrative with the feeling that these stories about him even demean his status as a true prophet of Israel. They consider the picture given of him here to be rather that of a performing magician than of a great prophetic servant of God raised up for a decisive task in the history of the people of God.

We repeat again our belief that the writer selected from his sources not only what he believed to be reliable information about Elisha, but also what in his estimation proved him to be a true man of God in the age in which he lived. These stories were all fondly remembered, recorded and circulated to vindicate the faith of these companies of prophets and the remarkable service Elisha gave them. They are a confession of faith in God's unfailing goodness and care for his trusting people in times of crisis. The needs of those who commit themselves wholly to him will be fully met; sometimes even by miraculous intervention! God will never let his people down.

The simple trust and piety of those people has never become out of date. Jesus, speaking of God's fatherly care for us, told us to take no thought for tomorrow, and then gave the assurance that if we strive first for the Kingdom of God and his righteousness, all the basic needs of life that make the people of the world so anxious in their striving, will be given to us (Matt. 6:25–34). It is in response to such aspects of his teaching that others now and then, here and there, have felt especially called to different forms of work in his name depending entirely for their financial support on what will come to them from friends and answers to prayer. Incidents in the lives of George Muller and Hudson Taylor, for instance, tell of critical situations in their work like those arising in these stories before us, saved by miraculous and last minute interventions by God working through some inspired human agency.

Skinner in his commentary on Kings remarks that 'much of Elisha's prophetic activity takes place on the lower levels of life'. He was referring especially to these present stories. Reading through the Bible we are continually reminded of

God's concern to control and direct the great affairs of human history. We see him at work controlling the migration of nations, directing the decisions of emperors, kings and great public figures, deciding the fate of their armies, controlling clouds, the waters of the sea and earthquakes. Here it is brought out that in ruling this universe his loving and marvellous concern reaches down to the ordinary and mundane affairs of daily life — to what happens in the cookhouse and storeroom of a little community, to what can happen to the borrowed axehead of a poor student volunteer, over-zealous in the way he does his work. It is the kind of concern Paul assures us about when he encourages us at one point in his letters to pray: 'Do not worry about anything, but in everything by prayer and supplication with thanksgiving let your requests be made known to God' (Phil. 4:6). Nothing is trivial to God if it makes us anxious. Are we not on the level at which Elisha was so greatly helped by God when we are engaged in tasks that might not seem to be directly spiritual (like that of catering for a Sunday School party) or directly political (like that of preparation for a small house group study on the Virgin Mary)? And are we not meant to understand that the help we are seeking in our prayer for such matters is that of the same marvellous power as raised Jesus from the dead?

From Jesus to Elisha — and vice versa

It is occasionally suggested to us, in reading the Gospels that Jesus at times in fulfilling his ministry quite consciously reproduced features from the ministry of the prophet Elisha. For instance, as well as Elisha, he marvellously multiplied a few loaves to feed many, then, when he went to Nain to raise the widow's son, he had Elisha in mind, for Nain was then the place name for Shunem where Elisha had raised the dead child. We ourselves have here already noted how Jesus shared Elisha's concern to give help to people, struggling to please God in the midst of the mundane difficulties and affairs of ordinary life. Following such clues, we have concentrated in this study on moving also from Elisha to Jesus, from the Old Testament to the New on the same low level of affairs where, nevertheless, important decisions in life are often made.

(1) 'Death in the Pot'

A zealous worker in the service of God found a job in the cookhouse of one of the communities where the prophets lived together. His task was undoubtedly important at that particular time because the land was in the grip of famine and food was scarce. Our man, full of zeal for God, determined to show it through his work in the kitchen. He was sent to collect herbs for the main meal of the day. This was cooked in one great pot. But he was a stranger to those parts around Gilgal. Perhaps he came from the north country where wild melons flourished and were much used for cooking. In his search for herbs he saw a plant that looked like wild melon. This plant, according to some commentators, is called colocynth. It grows abundantly by the Dead Sea and produces a fine-looking fruit, but it is, nevertheless, deadly poison. The man thought that these poisonous fruits were wild melons. He shredded them into the pot. In the middle of the meal the cry of alarm and despair was raised on all sides. Poison! Death! The precious rations were not only spoiled but there was the danger that those who had partaken might come to harm. It was a tragic mistake which might have had far-reaching effects, caused by the enthusiasm of the man who had committed it. Death in the pot!

As Elisha, by the power of God, was able to purge out the poison from the pottage which this zealous servant had made and cover over his mistakes, so Christ's miraculous power can cover over the mistakes we all make in his service. We can think of how Jesus, on two occasions, corrected the mistaken zeal of his followers in a most kindly way. On one occasion, the temple tax-gatherers asked Peter if his Master paid the temple tax. Peter said, 'Certainly, he will pay it.' It was a mistake. Jesus was the Lord of the temple, and certainly did not need to pay any temple tax. He rebuked Peter again gently for his mistake, but he saved the awkward situation by making a fish come from the depth of the sea with a coin in its mouth, so that the tax was paid in a manner that in no way obscured his lordship.

Thus Peter was rebuked, and yet his mistake was covered over. On another occasion the soldiers were coming to take Jesus by force, and one of His disciples, Peter, drew a sword, saying, 'Lord, should we strike with the sword?' He struck the servant of the high priest and cut off his ear. Jesus said, 'No more of this!' He touched the ear and healed him (Lk. 22:49–51).

We need the assurance which such stories can bring us when we think over the follies we have committed sometimes through our attempts to serve Jesus Christ. For many of us the enthusiasm of our early days of Christian service was often marred by misdirected zeal and by a way of approaching other people more likely to do harm than good in the service of Jesus Christ. As Church leaders we can spoil our influence by lack of tact. As teachers we can mix the truth at times with dangerous falsehood. As parents we can make psychological mistakes in dealing with our own children. At times we may think we are doing our best. A year or two later it is seen perhaps that the decision we made was the worst one possible and has done harm. How easily we become confused in the service of Jesus Christ — and our shortcomings can be devastating in their potential effects!

Yet Jesus was there in the days of his flesh to restrain his disciples and cover over their errors, and he is with us today. Through the miraculous power of Jesus Christ within his Church, God can use our service though it be mingled with mistakes. He can separate what is good in our influence and service from what is bad. He can counteract evil and ensure that there is no mistake irretrievable. He can take the mess of poisoned pottage and use it in his service.

(2) Only a Little for Too Many!

One day during a period of famine a farmer from the surrounding district, no doubt at great sacrifice, brought a present of food for the college of prophets. He seems to have announced confidently that he had brought a dinner of fresh loaves and barley and corn for everyone. Elisha told some of the prophets to go and help to unload it. There was some excitement among the men at the thought of a good meal.

But when they saw what the man had actually brought there were cries of dismay, and Gehazi, Elisha's servant, made a sarcastic remark. Twenty loaves and a little barley to feed a whole college!

It was a ridiculous situation, but Elisha insisted that inadequate though the offer might seem the meal was to be proceeded with. What the man had brought had to be set before the whole company. And the miracle happened. The man's sincere offering, though apparently inadequate to meet the situation, was sufficient and much was left over.

How like we are to this man of Baal-shalishah! For the sake of Christ we bring all we can to our service in the Church and the world, but how inadequate is our effort! Our own powers and talents and resources always seem ridiculously and depressingly short of what is needed for the task God has set us. There are those who feel so inadequate for the task that they never attempt anything for Jesus Christ. They draw back before they start, because they know they do not have the resources required.

Yet precisely at those moments when our powers fail through our inadequacy, Jesus Christ is there to save the situation from failure and ourselves from disgrace. If we would only from the start offer what we have to him, we would find that in a multitude of ways he can somehow take it into his hands and make it sufficient for a task greater than we ever dreamed of accomplishing.

There are two miracles of Jesus which illustrate this. One is the healing of the epileptic boy. While Jesus was on the Mount of Transfiguration a father brought his child to the disciples to cure. But they were unable to accomplish the task. They were beaten by the difficulty of it, and a partly hostile crowd gathered round. There was a disputation with the scribes who were watching their futile efforts. It was a miserable scene of failure in the service of Christ. But soon Jesus came on the scene, heard the sorry tale of failure, and cast out the demon. If our faith is in him, he will come to us even when we fail. He will step into our pathetic situation to vindicate his name, and to prove himself and his Church adequate in face of the most tragic demands of human need.

We can encourage ourselves also in the story of the feeding of the five thousand with the five barley loaves and the two fishes through the small offering willingly handed over to Andrew (Jn. 6:1–14).

(3) An Accident!

'*Now the company of prophets said to Elisha, "As you see, the place where we live under your charge is too small for us. Let us go to the Jordan, and let us collect logs there, one for each of us, and build a place there for us to live*"'. Their accommodation was inadequate and out of date. Elisha agreed. They collected the materials and tools and chose a site by the banks of the Jordan. Then an accident happened. '*But as one was felling a log, his axehead fell into the water; he cried out, "Alas, master! It was borrowed*"'.

In those days axes were scarce and valuable. Poor prophets did not possess many, and this particular one had been borrowed. A vexing and most unfortunate accident! It is the kind of thing that sometimes happens in Christian work. When we build for God the work can be spoiled not only by our own mistakes and inadequacies but also by sheer accidents that are beyond our control. Time and time again in the lives of great Christian enterprises there has come a crisis, when something we are tempted to describe as an evil fate seems to have stepped in to threaten all success.

Elisha acted quickly.

'*Then the man of God said, "Where did it fall?" When he showed him the place, he cut off a stick, and threw it in, and made the iron float. He said, "Pick it up." So he reached out his hand and took it.*'
We can take this miracle as a sign that God can overcome all that would spoil our plans and interfere in our work. It is a sign that God will allow no chance accident really to harm the work of his Kingdom. There is no such thing as chance to those who believe that all things work together for good to those who love God (Rom. 8:28). For Paul even the work of the Devil could be taken up by God and made to contribute to the building up of the Kingdom. Jesus' friends once suggested to him that if he went up to Jerusalem he might meet an untimely end. 'Are there not twelve hours in the day?', he said. 'If any

one walks in the day, he does not stumble' (Jn. 11:9). To Jesus there is a day for our work. Twelve hours are appointed to us. If God is with us in that time, there can be no stumbling and no accidents. Therefore we must not imagine that in the course of our service of God anything can happen that might be outside the scope of his providential care.

These three little miracles are messages of great encouragement to those who are seeking to serve God. Their message is, 'Let us not grow weary in well-doing, for in due season we shall reap, if we do not lose heart' (Gal. 6:9). Their message is, 'In the Lord your labour is not in vain' (1 Cor. 15:58). Our labour may seem to be in vain. It may seem to become spoilt by mistakes, shortcomings and accidents. But it is not in vain. Let us go to our work for Christ joyfully, remembering that he can turn poison into sweetness, he can turn our little offering into abundance, and he is always there to watch in the catastrophes that come upon us. He can make the lost axehead to swim.

Note

The Elisha Stories (3) — The Element of Offense
'The Miracles of Elisha' observes Jacques Ellul, 'are of every order, quality and dimension. We are often restive, full of doubts and ill at ease in face of these miracles which often seem to be miracles of poor quality to Christian piety'.

It is suggested that such as these stories now before us were given this final shape as remembered incidents from his life, were told and re-told within the fellowship of the various companies of prophets among whom he had spent much of his ministry. The miraculous element would arise out of the imaginative desire of his admirers and followers to enhance his reputation and stress how closely they could claim to have had such a great saint associated with them. The story of the floating axe-head, for example, could have arisen out of a fondly remembered occasion when he showed extraordinary skill locating and raising an axe, lost deep in mud, by probing and manoeuvering with a long pole. The healing of the poisoned pottage could have had its basis in an incident in which, by his superior knowledge of the potency of the herbs involved, he was able to persuade a hesitant group that the meal they had superstitiously refused to eat was, after all, wholesome.

The story of the multiplication of the loaves and the grain could have arisen out of the memory of another occasion when he had stifled rude complaints over the inadequacy of a well intentioned farmer's food-gift for a community meal, and persuaded everybody to appreciate the generous intention and to feel satisfied.

Several important considerations should affect our decision on this matter. Wilhem Vischer has suggested that Jesus had Elisha in mind when he replied to John the Baptist's query from prison as to whether or not he really was the Messiah. Jesus recognized that John himself was indeed the second Elijah who was prophesied by Malachi (Mal. 4:5) to appear in the world just before the Messiah and to be his herald. The Baptist had preached that Jesus was indeed the Christ, but in prison had fallen into doubt and was asking for reassurance. He had expected that by this time there would be more world-shaking and spectacular signs that the Kingdom of God had really come. Jesus in reply tried to reassure him by asking the messengers to tell him some of the pastoral miracles he had engaged himself in doing and added: 'Blessed is anyone who takes no offense in me' (Matt. 11:1–6). Vischer suggests that Jesus is here telling John that he was deliberately for a while conforming to the pattern of ministry followed by Elijah's successor Elisha. John in the meantime must seek no more than these low-level signs that he was indeed the true messianic successor of Elijah!

We have already referred to Jesus' visit to Nain where he gave a deliberate sign that he was following in the footsteps of Elisha, and we can think of his endorsement of two of our present studies in his own miracle of the feeding of thousands, and in giving the sign of the coin in the fish's mouth. Moreover there is the changing of the water into wine at Cana. Certainly each of these stories when understood in the light of his whole ministry can be shown as having profound theological meaning (see e.g. my *Gospel Miracles*, pp. 132ff. and *Gospel of John* pp. 36–39). Yet to convey such meaning, Jesus did not avoid the danger of being thought of as a wonder-worker. Was Paul referring to this among other signs of his limitation when he recorded that he 'took the form of a servant' (Phil. 2:7 A.V.)?

Points for Further Thought and Discussion

Many of us have learned to take pride in what we regard as our mainline tradition of Church conduct and worship. Do we sometimes deprive ourselves of the full enjoyment of the life open to us in Christ because we withhold ourselves from fellowship with those whom we regard as lacking the dignity and the status we associate with the best Church traditions?

We have heard men and women around us today testifying to God's marvellous provision of all their needs as they literally left almost everything in response to what they believed was his call to some specal mission. With our own custom in the Church of having a fixed salary and retirement allowance etc., are we in danger of losing our sensitivity to his calling and our entire dependence on him? Is our more routine system justified by New Testament precept and example?

Think of how much the teaching of Jesus encourages us to look for his providential care on what our study here pictures as 'the lower levels of life' (Cf. Mt. 6:25–33, 7:11).

Can you add illustrations to those given here of how Christ marvellously covers over, or cancels out, our immature failures in our dealings with life and with other people? And can you believe that even though evidence of the damage of such repented failure may linger on, all will be finally remedied in the great day to come?

Can you add illustrations to those given here of how God has used the most inadequate gifts of certain people for outstanding service in his Kingdom? Think of how this should encourage us to offer ourselves and what we have to him, and enable us to hope for Church renewal.

CHAPTER VI

NAAMAN — AND GEHAZI
2 Kings 5:1—27

The Narrative

Naaman, an important and wealthy Aramean military commander contracted leprosy and, hearing that a prophet in Israel was able to cure it, came to Elisha with rich gifts and great expectations. The cure, though it involved a series of humiliating experiences for Naaman, was effective and marvellous and brought him to faith in the God of Israel. Moreover, Elisha refused to accept the offer of payment or gifts. Gehazi, Elisha's servant, however, coveted what he saw when they were offered. Thinking to deceive both his master and Naaman he followed the departing caravan and persuaded the Aramean to leave a substantial payment with him, and then hid his spoil. Elisha, however, was able to discern what had happened and uttered a decree from God that he and his descendants should be plagued with the leprosy of Naaman.

Naaman — Disillusionment, Humiliation and Discovery

Naaman was in a position to enjoy the best that Aram could offer to its citizens. He was important in the King's court — '*a great man, and in high favour with his master*' (v. 1). No neighbouring land, he believed, had an economy so sound, a culture so splendid, or an army so strong. People from all around admired and coveted the treasures and silks it alone could produce in the world. When he travelled abroad he won deference with the magnificence of his entourage and his lavish gratuities for the least service given to him. He was justly proud especially of his own capital town, Damascus, with its two fine rivers Abana and Pharpar which rose fresh and cool in the mountains of Lebanon and then poured themselves out to irrigate and refresh a glorious oasis of trees and fertile country around the city, so that it shone like a white pearl in its green setting, against the dark background of rocky desert all around. It is said that when Muhammed viewed Damascus he refused to enter it, saying that there was only one Paradise for man, and he had decided not to enjoy his on earth.

One day, however, Naaman discovered that he had leprosy, and that in the midst of all the science, wealth and pomp of Aram there was no one who could even suggest a cure or give him any hope. Of course the king would have given him attendants, camels and caravans to escort him anywhere to look for one, and he sent messengers to find out where he should go. Everything drew a blank. But it happened that a young captive girl servant wanted to tell him about a prophet she knew of in Israel who had the power to cure even this dreadful plague. Strangely he was drawn to go.

Even the thought of going there to be cured offended his pride. He knew the place well from his war-time experience. The women when they were captured and enslaved certainly made good servants, but he could not help despising their god because he despised their land so much. Even Aram, he admitted, did not have much to boast about when it came to religious talk. He carried out his own worship in the temple of Rimmon his idol because at least he presided over a land that gave a man so much to live for!

His treatment from the moment of his arrival in Israel was shattering. He had brought silver and gold in abundance. He had made a display of the splendour of the world he belonged to: the chariots, horses, attendants, costly clothing. He had gone with the status of an important diplomatic envoy, with letters from his king. Of course he had gone straight to the palace of the king of Israel with no doubt that he would be received with honour, that the king would send an urgent message to his prophet, and that the man would cure him with an impressive ceremony. We are told how he thought it should have happened: '*He would surely come out, and stand, and call on the name of the Lord his God, and would wave his hand over the spot, and cure the leprosy!*' But the prophet did not even come to the palace and Naaman had to take his chariot and stately caravan to stand outside a humble dwelling house where they looked a most ridiculous sight. Nothing of any importance in Aram was of any worth in the eyes of this man of God! He did not even bother to come out and look. The letter from his king was left unread. Instead of a noble and dignified piece of ritual being performed, all he received was a curt message, '*Go, wash in the Jordan seven times*'.

His pride was shattered. He had been told to go to the Jordan,'*when Abana and Pharpar, the rivers of Damascus*', were '*better than all the waters of Israel!*' (v. 12). He had to do nothing hard, nothing noble, nothing costly, but merely wash and be clean! Consistently and ruthlessly he was being subjected to an ever-deepening process of humiliation calculated to tear away every shred of the superficial dignity that had helped him so far at least to hold up his head since the day his misery had begun.

Naaman could not have come through the ordeal but for his servants. It is to his credit that they cared for his welfare and could reason with him, knowing that he would listen. Having gone so far would this last easy step cost much more — and if it had been something difficult, would he not have done it? These more humble men seem to have grasped, before Naaman, that with Israel's God it is only the lowly and poor who are blessed while the rich are sent empty away.

The healing was immediate and the discovery was as sudden as the healing: '*there is no God in all the earth except in Israel*' (v. 15). Only here could such a word have ever been spoken! Only here could such a God have been met! What had happened to him was to involve a complete conversion of mind and values, and a transformation in his approach to life. Now he could go back home liberated not only from his own leprosy but from the deceitfulness of the world around him with its empty glory and false pride.

Today — Disillusionment, Humiliation and Discovery

In our life today we are worlds apart from life then in Damascus. Though Abana and Pharpar are still there in Syria as the Jordan is there in Israel, we can find only occasional traces of the other things we read about, only in museums. Yet the discovery that changed Naaman's devotion, life and thought is exactly the same as has changed our own hearts' devotion, life and thought — '*that there is no God in all the earth except in Israel!*' (v. 15). Moreover, as we read through the story with this in mind we ourselves have been able to find helpful similarities to our own experience in the process that led him to seek what he found, in what happened to him on his pilgrimage towards it, and in the effect it had on his future way of life.

Today many of us, if we are as fortunately placed as Naaman obviously was in Damascus, can find life as pleasant and good as he did before his trouble began. We, too, can find it healthy and wholesome without any thought entering our mind that we need much more. Immersion in the world can bring us into touch with much that is beautiful and noble, even uplifting in culture and nature. At times it can seem to reflect what some of its great thinkers have felt to be hints of a greater world beyond.

All this, we can believe, need not involve us in having anything to do with the Church of Christ or what it offers. We can find great satisfaction in our rich tradition of secular humanism, and there is a wealth of other religions that fit us more comfortably than traditional Christianity with its emphasis on self-restraint, discipline, and the Cross, and its strange talk at times of our need to be 'born again'.

Yet to some of us at least, experiences can come, and things can happen that begin to disturb us in our worldliness. We find ourselves personally let down too often and sometimes tragically. Enjoyments too readily grow stale with repetition. We begin to grow more conscious than before of the horrifying brutality, coarseness and degradation around the fringes of our life threatening indeed to take over our good world. We begin to wonder what has gone wrong with life around us and with ourselves. And sometimes to reinforce all this we can be further disturbed by echoes of the teaching of Jesus and the message of the Bible which can still filter through to us with searching questions about where we ourselves are going and the part we are playing: 'What shall it profit a man, if he shall gain the whole world, and lose his own soul?' (Mk. 8:36 A.V.).

A significant point in the Naaman story is that when such disillusionment began to come to him he discovered that a little child from Israel knew more about the solution of the deepest problem of his life than all the doctors and priests and nobles in Aram, that he heard the good news from her lips, too, and his life was changed. Jesus said 'I thank you Father, Lord of heaven and earth, because you have hidden these things from the wise and the intelligent, and have revealed them to infants; yes, Father, for such was your gracious will' (Mat. 11:25–26). The 'infants' who in their simplicity can repeat to us the texts about the love of God and the saving work of Jesus Christ or the hymns they learn in Sunday School about the green hill far away,

'Where the dear Lord was crucified
Who died to save us all,'

can tell us more about how to solve the deepest problems of our own lives and of the world's life than many of the great of this world. Perhaps that is why Jesus once set a little child in the midst of his disciples and said to them, 'Unless you change and become like children, you will never enter the kingdom of heaven' (Mat. 18:3).

For many of us the good news comes through preaching. 'For since in the wisdom of God, the world did not know God through wisdom, God decided, through the foolishness of our proclamation to save those who believe' (1 Cor. 1:21). It may be quite simple preaching, not entertaining or even eloquent. What matters is that it can tell us to look and move in the right direction.

When we look at the Cross to which the preaching finally points us there begins to happen for us the same kind of discovery as Naaman made on his journey to Israel. Jeremiah once summed up in unforgettable words the message he had to preach to the cultured and great in the world around him: 'Let not the wise man glory in his wisdom, let not the mighty man glory in his might, let not the rich man glory in his riches;

but let him who glories glory in this, that he understands and knows me' (Jer. 9:23–4). In Naaman's case his discovery of Israel involved him in a complete revaluation of everything he had gloried in. The culture of Aram that had formed his mind and given him his purpose in life, with its beauty and nobility, its pomp and show, its claims and boasts, had deceived him. It had failed him especially at the point of his deepest need. There was no god where it had led him to look for his god.

In our case, the Cross of Christ, as we look at it, and allow its meaning to possess our minds tends to make us ashamed of the false place of importance we have given to the world around us, the worth with which we have assessed it, and the trust we have put in it. Paul expressed what happened to himself, there before it, in words as memorable and powerful as those of Jeremiah: Far be it from me to glory except in the cross of our Lord Jesus Christ, by which the world has been crucified to me, and I to the world (Gal. 6:14 R.S.V.). As Augustine once put it, 'Before the Cross, all pride bends, breaks and dies.'

The final humiliaton comes when we discover, as the grace of God continues to deal with us, that what is wrong with us goes to the very root of our being. The waters in which we find ourselves being immersed as we submit to the Cross are the waters of re-birth as well as cleansing. What we ourselves have been, even at our best, is condemned by the very fact that, in the transformation that now takes place when we become a 'new creation', it is rejected. We have no ability to contribute anything towards even meeting our need. We need to be not simply mended or redirected, but re-born. We need to be saved from what we are.

But our discovery is as wonderful as was that of Naaman. 'Lo… this is the Lord for whom we have waited; let us be glad and rejoice in his salvation' (Is. 25:9). 'Everything old has passed away; see everything has become new' (2 Cor. 5:17)!

The Sequel

Naaman underwent in one moment as complete a conversion as that of Saul on the road to Damascus. When he came out of the water and found himself cleansed, he knew he had ceased to belong any more in heart and affection to Aram. He had ceased to belong to Rimmon the god of Aram. He had seen the emptiness of worship in Aram and the inability of its life and culture to meet the needs of men. '*I know that there is no God in all the earth, except in Israel.*'

But he had to go back and live in Aram. He had a home and a family there. His duty was to fulfil the contracts he had undertaken there, he felt that he must even bow with his master in the temple of Aram's god. Yet in all this his heart would be no longer in Aram but in Israel, and his true allegiance would be to the God of Israel. As a token of this he asked Elisha to let him take back two mule-loads of earth from Israel so that he might henceforth have a spot of Aram on which he would be able to worship and offer sacrifice to the God of Israel. He vowed henceforth to worship no other God but asked pardon if he should have to bow down with the king of Aram and his court in the now meaningless service in the temple of Rimmon. Full of gratitude, before he finally said farewell he wanted to leave a present of Aramean gold and silver and skills with Elisha. '*Please accept a present from your servant,*' (v. 15) he pleaded. But Elisha was firm in his refusal. He did not want it to be imagined by anyone that the help of the God of Israel could be bought for money.

It is at this point in the sequel to the story that we meet Gehazi, Elisha's servant, again. He was there and he saw the proposed present which Naaman displayed before his master. His eye caught the sheen of the silk and the glitter of the gold as Naaman packed it up, and had it stowed away in the chariot. He should have been proud of Elisha's action in scorning to take what Aram could offer — especially since it reinforced the witness that was to be given in the world to the healing and free grace of the God he served. Instead, he interpreted Elisha as acting merely out of sheer stupidity and narrow-minded prejudice. Even at the heart of Israel's religious life, and so close to one of its great prophets, he was a man without vision doing a service without meaning.

Therefore he ran after Naaman's chariot. No doubt inspired by his lust he went with extraordinary speed, caught up, and told his lie: '*My master has sent me to say, "Two members of a company of prophets have just come to me from the hill country of Ephraim:*

please give them a talent of silver and two changes of clothing"' (v. 22). It was no sudden downfall, but merely a revelation of what had been in his heart for years, always suppressed. But now before the chance of a lifetime he found himself unable any longer to resist. He hoped the pretence could continue. He hid his treasure, and '*went in, and stood before his master*'.

We are meant to have our minds arrested by the striking contrast now clearly brought out between Naaman and Gehazi. Gehazi is pledged to a job at the centre of the religious life of Israel, but his heart is not in the service of the God of Israel. His heart was in the gold and silver which Elisha was sending back to where it belonged, and he felt he would like to belong to the land which could produce such wealth. Naaman, called back to become immersed again in the day to day life of Aram, nevertheless belongs in desire and mind to the people of God in Israel. One other striking difference is that Naaman acts honestly, and openly confesses any compromise. Gehazi retreats into darkness and deceit. He stored the bags secretly and, as if nothing had happened, he resumed his place before Elisha.

The sequel to this part of the story is meant to shock and warn us —perhaps to make us feel uneasy. *'Elisha said to him, "Where have you been, Gehazi?" And he said, "Your servant went nowhere." But he said to him, "Did I not go with you in spirit when the man turned from his chariot to meet you? Was it a time to accept money and garments, olive orchards and vineyards, sheep and oxen, menservants and maidservants? Therefore the leprosy of Naaman shall cleave to you, and to your descendants for ever." So he went out from his presence a leper, as white as snow'* (as in R.S.V.).

The contrast is now heightened. '*Go in peace*', Elisha had said to Naaman. This 'man of the world', saved from its leprosy, was sent back to it in peace, even to remain blessed by God as he lives within it — because his heart was now fixed forever in Israel. '*The leprosy of Naaman shall cleave to you*', Elisha now says to Gehazi. He had apparently been a loyal churchman all his days. He had never polluted himself actively with the world's vice. But because his heart had been always oriented to what was alien to his professed faith, he comes under God's judgment. Naaman is pardoned even though he goes with others to the temple of Rimmon the God of Aram, for the two mules' burden of earth, on which he makes his sacrifice there, is a genuine sign of where his heart is. Gehazi is smitten even though he has never made one short visit to a night club or casino in Damascus.

'Where your treasure is there will your heart be also,' said Jesus (Mat. 6:21). We are meant by this story to ask ourselves the question. Where is our treasure? What do we count as our chief end, our chief gain, our main pleasure and happiness in life? Is that to be found for us in Israel or in Aram? We are not judged in the ultimate issue of things by where our job is. In this world as in Aram many men are compromised and what we do outwardly cannot always express where our heart is. Naaman had an exceedingly 'worldly' job, and even though his heart was not in it, he went through with it feeling that it had to be. Nor are we judged always by what our amusements are, though perhaps here there is more free choice to express what is in our hearts. But we are judged by where our *heart* is.

Where is our heart? How hard it is for us to tell where. God alone knows where a man's heart is and what a man trusts in. 'The heart is deceitful above all things, and desperately corrupt; who can understand it? I the Lord search the mind and try the heart' (Jeremiah 17:9, 10). How thankful we should be that in this very story there is a reminder that God has opened up for us a way to '*wash... and be clean*'!

Elisha on the Verge of Politics

The text of this incident with all its vivid and meaningful detail justifies our dealing with it in the way we have (see note). We must not however overlook that it helped to bring about an important development in the career of Elisha, and in the history of Israel. The prophet knew from early in his life that, at the culmination of his career, one of the chief tasks he had to do in the service of God was to involve him deeply in the political life of both Aram and Israel. Even while he concentrated on the pastoral and healing ministry he must have been alert for signs that God was opening up some way for this eventually to happen. Here was obviously a very important first contact with Aram! God was at work! We will discover in our next study that this incident was closely followed by another that took him even more decidedly into the heart of international politics now exactly in the direction to which he knew himself called.

Viewing this incident enables us to see the full importance of what Naaman's wife's serving maid did when she spoke to her mistress about Elisha. It is brought out clearly in the story that God was giving her at that moment an important place in working out his plan for his people and for the world. She was not in any way aware of the full significance of what she was doing, but there can be little doubt that she was trying to be helpful, and possibly from a deep and genuine desire to make known the love and power of God. When Jesus was being rejected by the people of Nazareth in their synagogue, he held up Naaman's obedience to the call of God, as an example to shame and warn them. Many other lepers in Aram could have been chosen for the privilege and the part God gave to him, but he alone was ready and willing to listen and to obey.

Jesus was there before the people of Nazareth giving them this same glorious opportunity in the Kingdom of God but unlike the serving girl and Naaman they were unaware and unconcerned that God was there and then seeking to enlist them in his service and Kingdom (cf. Luke 4:24–27). We ourselves are reminded here that we never know when life is bringing such a challenge and opportunity before us, and we, too, must be on the alert.

Note

The Stories of Elisha (4) — The Allegorical Element
I cannot avoid referring to my personal experience in interpreting this particular story. Though as a boy I was fairly well acquainted with most of the Old Testament stories, it happened that I had never heard, or heard of, this one. I heard it for the first time read in the church I attended shortly after I had undergone what was to me a conversion experience, involving through a sudden apprehension of the significance of the Cross, a total reorientation of my thought and life, and

a deep new appreciation of the Word of God and the salvation history recorded in the Bible.

I dd not understand the relevance of the sermon that was then preached on it, but my thoughts were almost entirely taken up by the story and I was excited by what I saw in it. Naaman was in many ways exactly like myself. The experience he underwent seemed exactly parallel in point after point to that which I had gone through. What had happened to me must have happened to people in the same way centuries before Christ and here was a writer to whom it had happened (like John Bunyan) constructing a marvellously interesting story to share his experience in the hope that others might recognise or enter it. Without feeling the need to look up any commentary on II Kings or discover anything more about Elisha or Syria (as Aram was then called in the A.V.) I preached on it, and I began to find out as I studied the story, the deep and subtle allegorical implications of the contrast between Gehazi and Naaman in the sequel.

In view of the almost unanimous disapproval of allegorical interpretation in evangelical books on Biblical nterpretation, I was glad to note that Wiseman in his recent commentary on this story quotes with approval the opinion of R. L. Cohn that the story is an 'apt example of Biblical narrative in which art and theology are symbiotically related'. I have, of course, become more and more certain that here we have history as well as allegory, and that the story is placed here to be read as an important historic event in the life of Elisha and in the development of the relations between Aram and Israel. 'The story' as one commentator puts it, ' bears in itself the impress of historical genuineness by virtue of its simplicity, its moderate statements, its numerous characteristic details. To invent such a story is impossible'. Here we have a quite marvellous blend of fact and symbol. Earl Ellis, acknowledging that Old Testament events can be typical of things to come in the New Testament uses the striking phrase: 'God writes his parables in the sands of time'. We have to be aware that God sometimes embeds allegory in salvation history as well as typology. Some of the other stories of Elisha we believe are in places designedly provocative of allegorical interpretation (see note in *Readings in I Kings* p. 117).

Points for Further Thought and Discussion

What Naaman stated about there being no other God is re-echoed here and there in the Bible (e.g. Isa. 45:18, Deut. 4:35). Do you agree with this affirmation, and does it reflect the teaching of Jesus? In view of the present day concern for dialogue and common worship with other religions how are we to interpret these texts?

Elisha, as we have seen, often showed himself friendly and eager to help others. Why do you think he was so unaccommodating and distant with Naaman?

Think of how Gehazi's fault and Elisha's condemnation of him helps to reinforce and interpret Jesus' words in Mat. 6:22-23 (refer especially here to A.V.).

Is it possible for a Christian to live and work in this present world around us without sometimes being involved in having to compromise in some matters? Can you think of limits you would set to the kind of job a Christian can accept, and what about amusements? Read Paul's positive approach to what is good in the world (in Phil. 4:8). Compare with 1 John 2:16, and explain.

Was Elisha right to refuse Naaman's gift? Compare his later apparent acceptance of a gift from the King of Aram (2 Kings 8:9). Try to explain. Do you think that the Christian witness of the Church today is sometimes hindered by its acceptance of gifts or patronage from some sources?

CHAPTER VII

THE TERRORIST CAMPAIGN
2 Kings 6:8-23

The Narrative

The King of Aram tried to wear down morale in Israel by terrorist raids at strategic points. He found that it was the intelligence supplied by Elisha to the leaders of Israel that prevented their effectiveness. Angry, he sent an expeditionary force to capture the prophet himself. Elisha by prayer and miraculous skill was able to foil its purpose and managed to manoeuvre it into surrender to the army of Israel at Samaria, where he was also instrumental in persuading the King of Israel to a remarkable display of mercy towards his captured enemy. The whole incident is to be read as the account of how Elisha attained fame both in his own country and in Aram, and contains also an illustration of his continuing pastoral care towards a young servant on the battlefield.

An Open Door

As his prophetic ministry took its course, Elisha must have wondered when a decisive opening would come to him to enter the world of power politics. He had been called to complete the destruction of Baalism that had threatened to destroy everything that had been of real worth in the life of the nation. Elijah on Carmel had broken its power, but it was still there in the land — a strong and dangerous influence. The final purge was planned to begin and God's final judgment was to fall when Hazael became King of Aram and Jehu was ready to become

King of Israel. Elisha's task was also to be there, somehow at the centre of political affairs, watching for the time to become ripe, and to speak the word that would make it happen.

This present chapter is the story of how with remarkable suddenness he found himself almost catapulted into the place God meant him to occupy, with all the avenues opening up before him for the important task to which he had been called. It was as if God had set before him an open door (Rev. 3:8). We are forced to notice that it was without any initiative on the part of Elisha, and through happenings entirely beyond his devising or even control that this important change took place in the direction of his career. God was obviously there controlling every human decision, working powerfully and marvellously through every detail, and shaping the situation, to give Elisha his great opportunity, and yet Elisha at least at first was unaware of the direction things were taking, and merely yielded himself to circumstances.

It was the King of Aram who was the active human agent in the working out of the plan. He set everything in motion and gave it fresh momentum when new development was required, though certainly he had no idea that he might be playing a part in fulfilling any purpose of the God of Israel.

The King was indeed motivated by his intense hatred of Israel. He was angry and frustrated that his costly attacks in open warfare had failed badly. He therefore changed his policy in conducting the long-drawn-out war. During a pause in hostilities, instead of mustering an army to conduct a further frontal attack, he had decided to wear down the morale of his enemy by resorting to a series of carefully planned terrorist raids by specially trained forces. They were to be sudden, unexpected in both timing and place, devastating in their toll of lives. Stealth and surprise were vitally important. The use of spies was important before the plans were finalised.

He had not realised while he was planning the whole campaign that he was playing into the hands of one man in Israel who was in a position to wreck it. Elisha, the prophet and healer to whom he had sent Naaman, was closely in touch with more sources of confidence and information in Syria than all the professional spies he himself sent to glean in Israel. Before the campaign began Elisha knew of its being planned.

He naturally yielded to his patriotic instinct, collected as much information as possible and passed it on to his own administration. They soon learned to depend on him for more and more intelligence and were invariably able to foil every plan of the enemy.

Of course as time passed Elisha began to realise that now at last God was opening up the way for him to do what had been pressing on his mind. He was winning the respect of the powers-that-be in Israel. Even the King was beginning to consult him. He was being brought into close touch with the army. (Might he not possibly have begun to meet and assess an aspiring young officer called Jehu?)

'Are there not twelve hours in a day?'

In this developing situation the next decisive step also was taken by the King of Aram. Frustrated and angry he held a council of war. Who could be the traitor? When they suggested Elisha's name, aroused to fury, he declared war on the prophet himself and made plans for an attack on his person with '*horses and chariots ... and a great army*' (v. 14). They made sure that this time evasion would be impossible. They discovered his exact location, attacked with stealth and with invincible strength. '*They came by night, and surrounded the city*' (v. 14). The King of Aram, however, then found himself beaten this time, not by Elisha but by the strange and miraculous providence of God. He was soon to learn that when the God of Israel had made his plans, and had sent a prophet to carry them out, the man, like Moses before Pharoah, was invulnerable.

We must pause to admire Elisha's serenity of mind at this moment of dire danger. He was upheld of course by his unshakeable conviction that when God had a work for anyone to do nothing could ever be allowed to stand in the way of its being done. It was the kind of faith that found its expression in one of Israel's great Psalms:

'Why do the nations conspire,
    and the peoples plot in vain?
The kings of the earth set themselves,

and the rulers take counsel together,
against the Lord and his anointed ...
He who sits in the heavens laughs:
the LORD has them in derision' (Ps. 2:1–4).

It also was given perfect expression by Jesus as he explained his fearlessness to his disciples as he was leading them on the way up to Jerusalem, 'are there not twelve hours of daylight? Those who walk during the day do not stumble, because they see the light of this world' (John 11:98). Elisha understood that perfectly. Exactly one day is appointed by God for each man's work. Neither he himself nor any other can lengthen or shorten it.

Elisha himself gives us a further clue to the extraordinary peace and presence of mind which came to him in this crisis. The vision he had had on the other side of Jordan, in answer to Elijah's last prayer for him, was recalled. He saw himself surrounded by heavenly '*horses and chariots of fire*' ready to fight on his side (vv. 16–17), and he was given again as he had been given then an unshakeable sense of the immediacy and the concrete reality of the help from God of which such visions are given to assure us. Jesus himself, we remember, derived the same kind of confidence from a vision which he described as that of 'more than twelve legions of angels' which his Father could send immediately he appealed for their help (Mat. 26:53).

As we read through the marvellous sequel to the attack they made in the morning it becomes clear that it was not the King of Aram who really presided over the war council that decided to attack Elisha, but the God of Israel, for Elisha's victory, and the exact way in which it was accomplished was even more decisive in enhancing his stature than any of his previous intelligence efforts, and this time it was in Aram as well as in Israel that he was to win the resulting esteem.

The Prayer and its Answer

When God made use of any form of miracle to rescue the people of Israel from their dangers and from the threats of their enemies, he normally used the simplest way possible, and avoided any unnecessarily extravagant display of the supernatural. We believe, therefore, that it was not the intention of the author who handed on this story to demand of his readers the belief that on the stroke of Elisha's sudden prayer each soldier in a whole great army was immediately struck by physical blindness, and that the whole body of men was then impelled under such blindness to march in orderly direction under Elisha's command. There are other ways in which to interpret the 'blindness' and to imagine the expeditionary force to have come under the prophet's control.

We believe that Elisha's prayer, '*strike this people, please, with blindness*' (v. 18) was inspired by the memory of the kind of thing God had at times done within Israel's history when he had rescued them from enemies who had overwhelming force (see note). He had often plagued their leaders' minds with illusions about threatening dangers to their safety, and spread corresponding panic among their ranks, so that they became inclined to flight and surrender.

An important point in the story is the contrast between the 'seeing' of Elisha's servant described in verse 17, and the 'blindness' of the Aramean army here under review. Since the 'seeing' he prayed for his servant obviously refers to insight of mind and a power to grasp all the important factors in the situation before him, the 'blindness' likewise, which he prayed for the Arameans to have, was confusion of mind, and an inability to grasp the real situation around them.

God, we believe, answered exactly this prayer. Elisha was inspired in a series of astute manoeuvres, completely to outwit the Aramean leaders, now easily duped and deluded, the whole force became so confused as entirely to lose their sense of proportion and to give way.

Bishop Hall, always conservative and believing in his comments, describes what happened in his own typical language: 'To all other objects their eyes are clear, not through darkness but through misknowledge; they shall see and mistake both the form and the place. He that made the senses can either hold or delude them at pleasure ... No sooner are they in Samaria than their eyes have leave to know both the place and the prospect.'

Elisha's Moment

We are meant to notice among the miracles recorded in this chapter, the conversion of the mind and whole attitude of King Jehoram towards Elisha. We can understand why, up till this present series of events, he had kept the prophet at a distance. At their first meeting he had been publicly insulted by the man, and he could recall too the fiasco in which that expedition had resulted. He had taken no interest in his ministry of helping and healing. It is noticeable that when Naaman came to his palace to seek healing in Israel no thought came to Jehoram that Elisha might be the man for the job (cf. 2 Kings 5:7). But his estimate of the man had begun completely to change as Elisha proved himself during the terrorist raids. And now when he suddenly found himself faced by further indisputable evidence of his extraordinary capabilities — the whole Aramean force there trapped and under his power! — all his reserve towards the prophet completely broke down. He must, surely in the days to come make this man a trusted counsellor, and even though he was longing to seize the opportunity for revenge that lay before him, nevertheless in the impulse of the moment he felt drawn to take Elisha's advice. '*Father, shall I kill them? Shall I kill them?*' (v. 21).

We will soon have to admit that this warm attitude towards Elisha was quite short lived. Jehoram, after all, was at heart devoted to Baal and before long the superficiality of his friendship with Elisha will be brought out during the siege of Samaria. But it lasted long enough to assure Elisha a stable place of influence among the leaders of his nation so that he could do the work for which God had raised him. In using people for his purposes God does not need to bring about within them any deep change of heart. When Darius raised Daniel, or Pharaoh raised Joseph, to places of influence in their kingdoms neither had experienced any wholehearted conversion to the God of Israel. Even a superficial impression or a momentary mood is sufficient for him to work through. 'The king's heart is a stream of water in the hand of the Lord; he turns it wherever he will' (Prov. 21:1).

Faced with the question put to him by Jehoram, Elisha would realise that on a day when so much else was being put in his way here was a further great opportunity being given to him by God. If he treated these Arameans with decency and tact, their king whom he had so angered could perhaps be won over, and a way would be opened up for him to play the part God had for him in that very land. Even though such pragmatic and prudential considerations may have been in his mind, the argument Elisha used with Jehoram when he asked him to treat them with generosity is remarkable. He argued that these people had been brought under the king's power purely by the miraculous providence and grace of God. He had not even won the right to make prisoners of them by defeating them in battle. This power had been given him by the grace of God. Let him therefore not use it in a way that rejected the same grace of God! Let him set before them 'a *great feast*' and send them home!

Here is one of these instances in Old Testament narrative where the behaviour of those led by God comes remarkably close to the ideal set before us in the New Testament. We, too, at times, find people around in situations similar to that of the Aramean soldiers in this incident. They are suffering deeply and sometimes have been exposed to public shame and humiliation —because of some sin or act of folly. It is so easy and natural for us to 'smite them' as Jehoram wanted to do and it is in our power to do so. We can gossip and spread the story and add our harsh judgment. We need, however, to remember the grace that God has shown to ourselves. The apostle Paul wrote to the Galatians, giving advice in the case of a member of their fellowship who had been caught in the act of doing something wrong, and was now publicly humiliated and shamed, with no defence. 'Restore him,' he wrote, 'in a spirit of gentleness. Look to yourself, lest you too be tempted. Bear one another's burdens, and so fulfil the law of Christ' (Galatians 6:1, 2). 'If your enemy is hungry, feed him' (Rom. 12:20). 'Pray for those who persecute you' (Matt. 5:44). 'Never avenge yourselves, but leave it to the wrath of God; for it is written, "Vengeance is mine, I will repay, says the Lord"' (Rom. 12:19).

The astonishingly kind treatment seemed to have an appeasing effect within the bitter conflict between these two enemies. At least '*the Arameans no longer came raiding into the land of Israel*'. It was by no means permanent, but it was regarded by the historian as worthy of bringing to his readers' notice that the example of such kindness can be worth following.

An Incident in Pastoral Care

We are not surprised to find Elisha, at the very time when he was engrossed in military affairs, able to give his concern for a few moments at least, even on the battlefield, to counselling and calming his servant when he heard his frightened cry, '*Alas, master! What shall we do?*' (v. 15). The pastoral instinct was always there and we will find him again many years later, on his death-bed, sought out for personal help by a worried king, and addressed as a 'father' in God (2 Kings 13:14). His immediate reply to his attendant in face of the surrounding enemy was to repeat some of those words of assuring exhortation that were part of the pastoral tradition of Israel: '*Do not be afraid*'. Abraham, Moses and Joshua had all heard God speaking such words to them and had passed them on when they had wanted to comfort others. Elisha went further. He spoke about his own experience and tried to share with his young attendant what was bringing such great confidence to himself there and then. He confessed the faith that had been his mainstay as a servant of God during the years of his ministry: '*There are more with us than there are with them*' (v. 16).

He was certain his message was from God, spoken out of genuine concern. He tried to be as convincing as he could. But even as he was speaking he was conscious of how far short his words were falling. How could mere words, however clearly spoken, and expressing the most earnest wish, open the heavens before the eyes of another, and give him the power to see beyond the earthly scene? Yet God, he knew from his own experience, had the power to do for his friend what he had already done for himself with Elijah by the Jordan (2 Kings 2:10-12). He therefore prayed, '*O LORD please open his eyes that he may see.*' Immediately the answer came: '*the LORD opened the eyes of the servant, and he saw*' (v. 17).

Our work in the Church today as pastors, preachers, and teachers involves us at times in the same kind of difficulty as faced Elisha. We, too have occasionally to point people to look at what is beyond the range of ordinary human perception. We often have to preach and teach about things and truths which cannot be seen or grasped by those we are speaking to, unless God opens the inner eyes of their minds to understand. We tell people the teaching of Jesus and the New Testament about the Kingdom of God, which is now in our midst and which has to be entered. We tell them of the power of the Holy Spirit to change lives. We speak to them of the Cross where we find salvation because the Lord has died for us. But these things are beyond the natural capacity and insight of those to whom we are speaking. Such truths must be *seen* if our teaching and words are to have meaning and relevance. Elisha's prayer is a model for all Christian preachers, counsellors, and educators (see further note).

Notes

On the Confusion among Israel's Enemies
There is the early promise that as his people begin to take possession of the land, God would spread reports about them which would cause other nations to tremble (Deut. 2:25). On one occasion Israel's enemies were confused by a 'panic sent by God' (1 Sam. 14:15), on another by a rumour preying on an already ominous sensitivity (Isa. 37:7), on another by imagining that strange sounds from beyond were those of a great advancing army (2 Kings 7:6).

On the Nature of the 'Seeing' Prayed for by Elisha
John Gray has an ingenious natural interpretation of this pastoral incident. It took place, he suggests, in a later historical context, during the course of a raid by Aramean border tribes whose movements were, with the knowledge of Elisha, being shadowed by an ambushing force of Israelites blocking their exit from the plan of Dothan while Elisha was enticing them

into the power of the main army of Israel. Elisha, here, was therefore simply trying to make his frightened servant fully aware of the extent of his tactical move.

We prefer to think more simply that Elisha, when confronted by the fear of his servant remembered the prayer Elijah uttered for him on that transforming experience near the Jordan where he himself was given insight into a whole new dimension of the world in which he was living.

Commentators who have tried seriously to grapple with the story differ as to what the final 'seeing' involved. Was it simply that the servant was suddenly given a stronger inner faith in the providential care of God? Was the vision of horses and chariots simply the 'thought image of his own mind'? Or did God give him some visible sign of his presence to his physical eyes? Or was the servant given the power to see beyond the earthly realm into a heavenly world?

We ourselves have stressed the fact that Jesus insisted that in the grasp of faith, along with a 'hearing' of what the word says, there should also be a 'seeing' of what the word points to (cf. Matt. 13:16, Mark 8:18).

Points for Further Thought and Discussion

'I have set before you an open door' (Rev. 3:8). We have interpreted the story here as of a series of providential happenings through which God opened the door for Elisha to be in a position in which he could begin to fulfil the main task in life which God had ordained for him. Do you find this relevant to the situation you yourself are in today? Is each of us to believe that God is controlling our affairs in this way?

When Jesus finally submitted himself to become the victim of our human brutality, he reminded Pontius Pilate that he really had the power to befriend him instead of crucifying him (cf. John 19:10–11). Think of the nature of the power that each of us has over the welfare and happiness of others, especially those with whom we are bound up closely in life. Are we living up to it?

The happenings of this chapter suggest that God at that time carefully controlled the thoughts and decisions of the kings involved. Do you think he does this kind of thing today? What does the New Testament suggest? (cf. John 19:10–11, Acts 12:5–7, 1 Tim 2:1–2). How important a place should prayer on this matter have in our Church and personal lives (cf. 1 Sam. 12:23)?

The pastoral incident in this story suggests that it was important for the boy to be enabled somehow to see what he heard about. Does this help us to understand what Jesus meant when he insisted that people must 'see' as well as hear? (cf. Mark 8:18, Mat. 13:16–17). Have you yourself had any experience of 'seeing' what is being talked about? Do you think that it is important?

Think of the question with which our discussion closed. Can we be truly efficient teachers of others (parents of children, pastors of the flock, teachers in Church clubs and classes) without the individual concern and prayer for each hearer?

What implications does this have for our Church work, ministry and Sunday worship?

CHAPTER VIII

THE SIEGE OF SAMARIA
2 Kings 6:24–7:20

The Narrative

We are given a picture here of harrowing scenes during a siege by the Arameans of Samaria. Elisha had persuaded the inhabitants to prolong their resistance to the enemy because he had prophesied a coming deliverance. Public opinion under the strain of waiting turns against him and the king tries to take his life. At the crucial moment the word comes to Elisha of immediate and marvellous deliverance. There are vivid details of how it happens, how news of it is brought to the city, and how judgment comes to those who refused to believe in the word of the prophet.

Human Nature under Stress

Aram and Israel are back at war. Samaria, Israel's capital city has been besieged for months by the Arameans. The citizens had been willing to endure prolonged and intense suffering because they were aware of how dreadful the consequences would be of surrender to such a brutal enemy. They were crying out for food. The black marketeers and war profiteers were growing rich. '*A donkey's head was sold for eighty shekels of silver, and one fourth of a kab of dove's dung for five shekels*' (v. 25). Perhaps they hoped the siege would continue until they had fully exploited the situation.

No doubt by the grace of God here and there under this siege some people rose to great heights of heroism and self-sacrifice. Others simply revealed what is worst in human nature. Some of the women of the nation lost all their fine feelings and in lack of natural affection descended below the level of the beast, and were not even ashamed. The king of Israel, the story tells us, met two women having a fight. One of them pled to him for justice, and on his enquiring what was the matter, she cried out: '*This woman said to me, "Give up your son; we will eat him today, and we will eat my son tomorrow." So we cooked my son, and ate him. The next day I said to her, "Give up your son, and we will eat him". But she has hidden her son*' (vv. 28–29).

Take away the grace of God, then the moral conventions that usually keep men and women respectable begin to disappear, and human nature behaves like that! We need not imagine that today we are much better than they. Here is a story about the nature with which each of us is born (see question). 'The grass withers, the flower fades,' cried the prophet (Isa. 40:7). By 'the grass' and 'the flower' he meant human nature as it is in every age. Winston Churchill once said in a speech: 'Certain it is that while men are gathering knowledge and power with ever-increasing and measureless speed, their virtues and their wisdom have not shown any notable improvement as the centuries have rolled on.... Under sufficient stress —starvation, warlike passion or even cold intellectual frenzy —the modern man we know so well will do the most terrible deeds, and his modern woman will back him up.' What people did when Christ was crucified was more significant of the capability of human nature for evil than even what took place during the siege of Samaria, and it shows up the true nature not only of that generation which crucified him, but ours too.

The King Reveals Himself

In the midst of these signs of moral degeneration there had arisen acute political tension. The people had been encouraged to hold on, and endure the extreme siege conditions because Elisha had spoken strongly against surrender, and had promised in the name of the Lord that deliverance would eventually come. His word had been convincing and many had trusted him. But now public opinion was changing. A growing majority were beginning to blame him bitterly for the evils that had piled up, one upon another. The king's loyalty to him had also come under strain. Up till now he had shown a half-hearted inclination to support the truth for which the prophets stood. He had early in his life removed from its prominent place a Baal pillar which he felt to be offensive though he had not destroyed it (cf. 2 Kings 3:2, 10:26). Since the beginning of the events of the last chapter he had given Elisha a prominent place in national affairs.

We must give him credit for some admirable features in the way he bore himself up till this point in the siege. He went about the streets of the beleaguered city among the people, showing concern, trying to sum up the situation, seeking to rally them to support the resistance. Moreover, in his reaction to the shock that came to him when he was approached to give his judgment in the sordid transaction between the two crazed women, he tore his royal robes. This gesture revealed that he had the habit of wearing sackcloth next to his skin as an expression of his personal identification with the sufferings of his people.

The shock, though it revealed an attractive aspect of his character, had nevertheless the effect of tragically plunging him completely into the unbelief which he had been obviously struggling hard to control. It must have astonished many who heard him when he now made a public renunciation of everything that Elisha had stood for, and a blasphemous vow to have the prophet executed before the day was out. '*So may God do to me and more, if the head of Elisha, son of Shaphat, stays on his shoulders today*' (v. 31). He sent off an assassin at all speed to carry out the execution and then with mounting anger he hurried after the messenger to see if he could overtake him. He wanted Elisha before he died to know the reason why he had been condemned. His crime was that he himself with all his false god-talk, alone had been responsible for all the misery that had come upon the city: '*This trouble is from the LORD! Why should I hope in the LORD any longer?*' (v. 33).

Elisha had, perhaps from the beginning of the relationship, suspected Jehoram of insincerity in his profession of faith, and before the king and his messenger had time to reach his house, he was given a prophetic intimation (cf. 8:12) of the king's approach and intention. He was sitting in fellowship with his elders when it came to him, and immediately he ordered them to bar the door to prevent the assault. His description of Jehoram is revealing: '*Are you aware,*' he said to the elders, '*that this murderer has sent someone to take off my head?*' (v. 32). In his eyes the king ('*this murderer!*') was now simply revealing what had all along been his true character.

Jehoram's reversal of religious loyalty proved now to be permanent and determined. Even though events suddenly took a turn in Elisha's favour and his desire for vengeance was thwarted, he showed no sign of repentance. He will hear Elisha's prophecy of coming good fortune with cynicism. It need not surprise us eventually to read that he finally cast his lot with the adherents of Baal and suffered their fate under the sword of Jehu.

Jehoram reminds us of Saul, the king whose faith for a time seemed to be strong and loyal, yet in the long run also proved to be temporary. When Jesus spoke the parable of the Ten Virgins (Matt. 25:1–13), he was warning us that even within his Church, there can be those of us whose profession of faith has all the outward marks of genuineness but which, in the long run, and under conditions of crisis and testing, can prove to have been all along deceptive. 'Examine yourselves' (1 Cor. 11:28) wrote Paul to the Christians in Corinth.

The Waiting Church and Prophet

Before we are further caught up in the swift movement and drama of this story, it is worth while pausing to take in the full significance of the picture given here of Elisha in his house with the elders gathered round him. It is of a prophet of God whose word from God has involved him in bitter conflict with the people he has been sent to serve and save — misunderstood, on the verge of rejection, and under threat of death. Yet, as Isaiah was at a difficult moment in his public career (cf. Isa. 8:11–16, see note), he is surrounded and supported by a few disciples whom God has drawn to him to give him fellowship and strength. These men might easily have given way before the growing community hostility towards Elisha. Their rations were as meagre and their sufferings as acute as those of anyone else. But God's grace kept them steadfast in the faith, and they strengthened each other in the fellowship they found as they continually gathered around him to seek with him the Word of God which they were certain would be given in God's good time to those who waited before him.

We are meant to appreciate what the presence of these few around him meant to Elisha. He had never before found himself alienated from the people he felt he belonged to. He had certainly been in such danger before — as at Dothan. There God had given him a marvellous vision. But here there was none. It was a new and severe test for him to have to wait so long on and on in such exhausting tension without any sign or word. But now, he was discovering, God was indeed with him as before. Indeed, the fellowship of these elders was as much a token of God's love and presence with him as any miraculous vision could be. The elders themselves are not waiting for any spectacular sign that God is with them but simply for the word which they believe will be given in time, for they knew that God had promised by such a word to save the city.

Throughout the Christian centuries the Church here and there and at varied times has re-presented this picture of a small, threatened but faithful congregation, forced to draw itself apart from an alien world and hostile forces of government. Its members and pastors are taking every precaution to defend themselves — locking the doors against attack! — while looking to God alone to save them. They are seeking courage, strength and guidance from the Word of God which they know they will hear through Holy Scripture. The voice of Christ, the Good Shepherd, they believe will show them the way and yet bring salvation to this world for which they pray. Perhaps in this Old Testament incident we have a picture relevant to the times that we ourselves as his Church today may be moving into.

The Word

The Word when it came switched the thoughts of everyone

who heard, away from the arguments for and against Elisha to one question alone: Was it or was it not possible? Would it or would it not happen? It heightened the tension by demanding immediate decision: '*Tomorrow*', it said. When it was announced, each had a straightforward and urgently pressing question to answer. They were being tested. They were going to be judged by the answer they gave, and they must give the answer here and now. To answer 'wait and see' meant they did not believe.

Because it said '*Tomorrow*' it enabled the King to control his ardent hatred for Elisha. It enabled him with dignity and confidence to postpone the execution. Just one more day! The things prophesied would never happen and then he would have a proven liar securely where he wished him!

The astonishing details with which the word was given, were calculated to bring more assurance to the disciples of Elisha than if there had been just a vague promise: '*Tomorrow about this time a measure of choice meal shall be sold for a shekel, and two measures of barley for a shekel, at the gate of Samaria*' (7:1). Certainly it was a severe test even for them. No miraculous sign was given to support such 'unbelievable' assertions, no explanation of how it could possibly come to pass. They had no word of any relieving army marching to their rescue. Yet such was the Word of God, and the prophet spoke it without a trace of hesitation in his voice. It was not credible that Elisha in any mood of doubt or in any haste to postpone the crisis could have himself conceived such an utterance. It must have come from God.

The Word of God always makes those who hear it free in their response to his love. One of the King's stewards laughed, and scoffed publicly at the message. '*Even if the Lord were to make windows in the sky, could such a thing happen?*' (7:2). Elisha there and then was moved to pronounce judgment, '*You shall see it with your own eyes, but you shall not eat from it*'.

The Four Witnesses

The miracle that seemed impossible to unbelief happened as God often made such things happen in those days. He did it with omnipotent ease and the whole affair had his unique signature. No spectacular intervention was necessary. It happened 'all in the mind'. The Arameans heard '*the sound of chariots, and of horses, the sound of a great army*' (v. 6). God had already put them in the mood which he once threatened to bring upon his own people if they persisted in disobedience: 'I will send faintness into their hearts ... the sound of a driven leaf shall put them to flight ... Though no-one pursues' (Lev. 26:36). Jacques Ellul rightly here suggests a thought worth our reflection: 'Here we had a victorious army, a devastating war, imperial politics, and then an echo; there is nothing left. God in heaven does indeed laugh to scorn the furious raging of the people' (Ps. 2:1ff.).

The sign that God had done this miracle, like the sign of the open empty tomb on the first Easter, required witnesses before its immediate purpose was fully achieved. Events continue to be moved by a chain of reasoning within the human mind. Four lepers live outside the city and they have become desperate to scavenge just what might keep them alive a little longer. They know it might cost them their lives if they went near the city, looking as if they might steal even a morsel. To approach the Aramean camp might mean death too, but now they have no other alternative but to take the risk.

When they find the camp empty they naturally think only of themselves. They eat and drink their fill and lay up for themselves as much as their many little safe hiding places can take of '*silver, gold and clothing*' (v. 8). But God is watching the time. Elisha's prophecy is to be exactly fulfilled. They begin to have a conscience and to indulge in a little self-centred moral reasoning: '*What we are doing is wrong ... if we are silent and wait ... we will be found guilty*' (v. 9). They even become uplifted by the thought of joy they could bring to the city in this '*day of good news*'. But they are cautious. They don't want to be overwhelmed in any great mob stampede. Perhaps they want to be given some credit for bringing the story. Perhaps here is an opportunity to ingratiate themselves with the King.

Judgment with Salvation

We are left to imagine the wild and hilarious celebrations when the mob arrived at the camp, and to picture for ourselves the people gorging themselves, hugging their loot and even fighting over it. Their city had been saved! The writer of the story is chiefly concerned to bring home to us not only that the word of salvation comes to pass but that the word of judgment was precisely fulfilled in all its details. We are told, therefore, that in the mad rush through the gate of the city when the news was first heard, the judgment pronounced by Elisha came upon the scoffer. '*It did indeed happen,*' the writer insists, '*the people trampled him to death in the gate*' (7:20 cf. v. 17).

The author of the narrative is even more concerned that we should note how Jehoram put himself beyond being dealt any longer with hope or mercy. It was exactly God's purpose that he should be the first confronted with the news and tested as to how he was to receive it. He now fully reveals himself. He cannot bring himself to face the possibility that it can genuinely have happened and becomes certain that it is a trap set by the Arameans! He calls a council to alert them of this fresh danger to their city. One or two remember Elisha's prophecy of yesterday. They want at least to risk the lives of five horses and then to explore the ground. The King in his continuing hardened scepticism refuses to send more than two to what he believes will be their certain death!

He is to be the last king of the house of Omri. Before we read of the tragic end of his life, we are here being given an explanation of what is to happen. Every way has been tried to bring him to repentance. In every cranny of his mind some remnant even of genuine compunction has been sought for — and nothing has been found.

Notes

The Historical Setting
It is pointed out by commentators that in this story (as in e.g. I Kings 20) the king involved is almost continuously referred to as 'the king of Israel', and that the editor of the book was quite free to apply it to the king of his choice. It is suggested by some that the famine context (see note on p. 106) and the note in 6:33 implying a long pause in the Arameo–Israel

hostilities, indicate that the incident belongs to a later reign than that of Jehoram, possibly Jehoahaz or Joash. We ourselves feel certain that the author's application of it is unquestionable. It serves to describe and explain Jehoram's apostasy, and it would have been quite uncharacteristic of any of the three following kings of Israel.

6:25 *'Dove's dung'* may have been used for fuel or, more likely, was a popular name for some kind of food like carob beans or wild onions. The cost of a donkey's head causes Bishop Hall to meditate sympathetically on the 'untoothsomeness' of such an 'impure creature'. 'That which the law of ceremonies had made unclean, the law of necessity had made delicate and precious; the bones of so carrion a head could not be picked for less than four hundred pieces of silver'.

6:28-29 *Human Behaviour under Siege.* The whole passage Deut. 28:53-57 speaks of how under the extreme conditions of siege and hunger, even the most 'refined and gentle' (and 'compassionate', cf. Lam. 4:10) men and women will behave exactly as these two in this incident. Cf. also Ezek. 5:10 and Lam. 2:20).

Elisha and his Elders — the 'Remnant'
As the great prophets of Israel began to find that their message was increasingly unpopular, and to discover that only a few around them seemed to respond to their call, they took assurance in the promise continually heard by them that no matter how deep and widespread Israel's apostasy might become, nevertheless under the worst circumstances God would ensure the presence around them of a faithful 'remnant' of his people. It might at times be only a few. The doctrine appears first in Amos (cf. 3:12, 5:3) where it is held that the existence even of such a few can be a sign of hope for the future (5:15). It became in Isaiah a central doctrine of hope as he faced the question of the future survival of the people of God (cf. Isa. 6:11-13, 10:20-23, 37:31-32). In such passages the 'remnant' is described as surviving the destruction of surrounding forests under the judgment of God but out of the surviving 'stump of Jesse' there is to grow the branch that will fulfil the messianic purpose for which Israel was originally called. At one point in his career, Isaiah was tempted to give

way to depression, and as he looked round on the small body of his disciples gathered around him he referred to them as 'signs and portents in Israel' (Isa. 8:18). They seemed to be signs that God was with him (8:10) and portents of a tribulation (8:19–22) that would characterise the future. Might he have been thinking then of this vivid picture of Elisha with his remnant? We have to remember that Elijah in his depression was assured of the invisible seven thousand who had not bowed the knee to Baal.

Points for Further Thought and Discussion

Was Jesus born with the same kind of human nature as could so easily, under stress, sink into the kind of behaviour we find described here? Some theologians have denied this. They have argued that while our own human nature was derived from what Adam became after the Fall, the human nature that Jesus was born with was the same as that which was given to Adam before the Fall. Other theologians (e.g. Karl Barth) disagree. They argue that the humanity which the Son of God was given from the womb of Mary was identical with our fallen humanity, and was kept at every stage of his life entirely free from sin by the grace and power of God. What do you think?

Jehoram (cf. 2 Kings 6:21) was obviously moved towards his temporary faith in God by his sheer admiration of the person and example of the great prophet. Can you think of some today whose faith has been inspired by such example and personal influence? Can this be a good beginning? Is it ever adequate?

Elisha and the gathered elders around him knew themselves to be in a desperate situation unless God's word came to them, and were no doubt praying with urgency that they might hear. Should we today be experiencing within our Church life something of this urgent hunger for the word and might the lack of such hunger be a reason why sometimes we do not hear it?

'This is a day of good news ... therefore let us go and tell' (7:9). Preachers sometimes isolate this text and use it to urge people to evangelism and missionary activity. Think of what it can say to us as it comes to us, as individuals and as a Church, in this isolated way. Think over the encouragement (or the rebuke) it can be to us that God used such vulnerable and despised people as the lepers to be such effective evangelists.

It is clearly shown in this story that the central 'miracle' was brought about simply by God putting thoughts and imaginations in people's minds (cf. 7:3—4, and 6—7). Do you think that this is often his way providentially to bring about (sometimes miraculously) his will in human history today? What encouragement can we therefore take, and how should this affect our praying?

CHAPTER IX

THE ANOINTING OF HAZAEL AND JEHU
2 Kings 8:1–9:13

The Narrative

The passage opens with a tribute to Elisha, since his political career is now moving towards its fulfilment and therefore its end. We are then told of how he himself goes to Damascus and of how he tried to fulfil his commission to anoint Hazael. We are then brought up-to-date with the history of Judah, being especially reminded of how the daughter of Jezebel had been married to Jehoram, King of Judah, and we are introduced to Ahaziah his son. We are told how Hazael begins to war against Israel at Ramoth-gilead. Jehoram, King of Israel, is wounded in battle there, retires to Jezreel where Ahaziah his cousin visits him and delays his return. To a meeting of discontented generals of Israel's army Elisha sends a young prophet to anoint Jehu as the future King of Israel.

Elisha — Agent of Judgment and Sign of Grace

In this section of the book, two important events are brought before us — the 'anointing' of Hazael to kingship in Aram, and of Jehu to that in Israel. Both are warlike and brutal characters. Hazael's task is to wage a punitive war on both Israel and Judah, so that it can register in their minds and memory that God will never tolerate again the pagan idolatry they have indulged in. Jehu's task is to take power within Israel by revolution and to purge the land from Baalism and all its adherents.

It was to Elijah that the call to anoint these two men was originally given years ago at Horeb (cf. 1 Kings 19:15–17). God had allowed a long time to pass before the way was finally made clear for the dead prophet's successor to fulfil them. God often shows himself 'slow to anger' (Ex. 34:6). He hates what happens when wars, international or civil, take place — the bloodshed, the brutalizing, the looting, the rapes, the bereavements and all the human agony. Might not the cause of the delay have been his hope that the eventual effect of what happened at Carmel, and the years of Elisha's gracious ministry of witness to his truth, might be to bring his people back to himself so that the judgment could be averted, and the purge become unnecessary? But in spite of everything Baalism was still there with a grip on some that threatened the whole future of God's purpose with his people. We have had clear evidence of its power as we have watched the career of Jehoram — and Jezebel was still there, proud and active!

We will find that after he fulfils these two tasks, Elisha's active career in politics is brought to an end. He had very many years still to live. No doubt he continued his pastoral ministry. Scripture is economical with its space, and records often only the few very significant things that happen in the otherwise full lives of those about whom it tells us (cf. John 21:25).

Before he finally brings his account of the active ministry of Elisha to an end, however, the historian here pays tribute to him by inserting a short incident that happened during the reign of one of the kings of Israel (8:1–6, see note). The Shunammite (cf. 2 Kings 4:8ff.) having been advised by Elisha to leave the country during a famine returned to find her estate occupied by others and came to the court to ask it back. She appeared there, by remarkable coincidence, at a time when incidents from Elisha's remarkable ministry were being talked about with fond appreciation, including what had happened in her case! He himself is not there, but his influence still counts. People are uplifted and thankful as they talk of him! We must keep this in mind as we read on through these coming dismal chapters about the judgments that are going to be triggered off by what he himself is now used by God to set in motion. Jacques Ellul pays a just tribute to his influence: 'It should always be remembered that God does not strike without healing, that he does not condemn without consoling, that he does not judge without the Gospel. During these years of testing Elisha is there. Elisha is the visible and active presence of God.... He is the sign and proof and witness that God has not abandoned his people. The test can be terrible but the prophet is there'. He becomes a living legend and even his political influence can again become strong. He lives on for many years and before he dies he is able to counsel and strengthen Joash the last king of the dynasty of Jehu (cf. 13:14-19). Jesus taught in his parable of the tares and the wheat (cf. Matt. 13:24-30, 36-43) that the good and gentle things of life, may for a time become obscured by harsher 'realities' which seem temporarily to blot them out, but they are there to be gathered up and harvested into the Kingdom of God when the final reckoning comes.

Elisha and Hazael

Now having proved by so many signs that God is faithful, kind and understanding Elisha has to yield himself into God's hands to become the agent of that other work that has also to be done. He must take responsibility for letting it be known that God is indeed jealous for his name, that when his people are deliberate and determined in their resistance to him he will by no means clear the guilty, and that this can involve even the visitation of the sins of the parents upon the children (Exod. 34:7, Deut. 5:9). Elisha was all the more reluctant to become involved in this task because he knew how God went about doing such a work. He used the kind of people most suited for the job on hand. As the work was being carried out he did not use them as controlled robots but as responsible persons, and while he was using them they always had freedom to be themselves and do their own thing.

Even before he set out on his mission to anoint them, Elisha was appalled at the thought of what might happen to the men, women and children of Israel when men like Hazael and Jehu were set loose on their task. Some of their victims would be his own friends. And what about his own family and the homestead at Abel-meholah? He hesitated. Yet he knew that God was waiting. The time had come, and he had to go.

He found the situation in Aram worse than he feared. Hazael was a trusted servant of Ben-hadad, the King of Aram. The King himself was ill and he sent Hazael to meet the famous prophet with a present and a question. Though Elijah had in earlier days refused Naaman's gift, he seems to have thought that as an act of pure courtesy he could not seem to reject this one. Indeed he seems to have been pleased to have been given such a welcome. It was a tribute to the Lord that a foreign King was ready to consult his prophet. Yet, gradually, as he looked at Hazael and grasped the situation before him he began to tremble at the possible consequences of what he had come to do. The example of Jeremiah can help us at this point to understand the feelings of Elisha. Jeremiah, at one time, confesses that by nature he too shrank from uttering the word God gave him to speak. He even hardened himself against it with rock-like resistance (Jer. 20:8), yet he found himself forced in the long run to go where God sent him, and to speak what God willed, for the word within him was 'like fire, and like a hammer that breaks a rock in pieces' (23:29). Elisha, likewise, horrified by what he knew his word would bring about, found himself simply compelled to be its agent.

During his life on earth Jesus was able to read the minds of people. He was able to predict their future path. He did this, for example, for Peter, Nathanael and Judas (John 1:42, 48; 6:64). Jesus 'knew what was in man' wrote John (John 2:25). This gift was sometimes also given to the Old Testament prophets whose ministry prepared for and fore-shadowed that of Jesus. Elisha had such a gift. Because he was able to read Hazael's mind, he spoke at first with what appears to us to be some confusion. '*Your son King Ben-hadad of Aram has sent me to you,*' said Hazael, '*saying "Shall I recover from this illness?"*' 'Elisha said to him, '*Go, say to him, "You shall certainly recover," but the LORD has shown me that he shall certainly die.*' (8:9–10) It seems as if Elisha knew he could not recover but he told Hazael to tell him he would! Did he really intend to deceive Ben-hadad? Some commentators overcome the difficulty by emphasising the fact that in some of the early manuscripts the message is altered to read: 'he shall certainly not recover'. John Gray makes the helpful suggestion that the words in question were meant to be conveyed rather as a friendly greeting than as a serious message.

We prefer to take it that when Elisha spoke, he did not really intend the message to be delivered to Ben-hadad at all, but was simply speaking out his thoughts before Hazael, partly in sarcasm, knowing well that the real truth could not be conveyed to the king by such a messenger.

Elisha's horror increased as his vision of the situation continued. The New English Bible gives an effective translation: '*The man of God stood there with set face like a man stunned, until he could bear it no longer; then he wept*' (v. 11). He recalled that Hazael was to be allowed by God to bring judgment on his own countrymen in Israel. He saw clearly that the man before him loved to wage war, to slay young men, dash little ones in pieces, and violate women! When Hazael asked Elisha why he wept, Elisha accused him of desiring to do such things, and Hazael unashamedly gave expression in his reply to the vile ambition in his heart. How could he do '*this great thing*'? To command an army in a victory which would lead to such plunder and slaughter — this to Hazael's mind would be to achieve the summit of earthly glory! But he said, '*what is your servant, who is a mere dog?*' (v. 13); how could he, a mere servant in the king's palace, ever hope to rise to such heights?

We can now observe and fully understand Elisha's reaction to the shameless cruelty of the man before him. How could anyone with even one spark of human decency or godly fear within him ever show any desire to be associated with such a person as this — even in the service of God? Elisha did not dare to disobey the Word of God. He had been told to speak the word which would make this man king of Aram, and he spoke it. '*The Lord has shown me that you are to be king over Aram*' (v. 13). Yet he could not bring himself publicly to side with him. He omitted to anoint Hazael. He would leave it with God, his gracious Master, to judge him if he were wrong. He was soon to hear that the word he had spoken was beginning to have the consequences he had dreaded.

Hazael, emboldened by Elisha's prophecy, murdered his king and obtained the throne of Syria. A dark shadow now hung over the lives of those in Israel who, because of their nation's impenitence, would die under the sword of Hazael.

The Task before Jehu

To enable us fully to understand the work of Jehu, the writer of the history has first of all to bring us up-to-date with the history of Judah, and he takes up several verses of the narrative in doing so. We learn that Baalism has within the course of only a generation deeply polluted its royal house too. Jehoshaphat its king whom we have already met on several occasions (and about whom we tend to have formed a favourable impression — 2 Kings 3:14) married his son Jehoram to Athaliah the daughter of Ahab and Jezebel through whom Baal had been given its deep foothold in Israel itself. We are not surprised to read that Jehoram of Judah also began to walk in the ways of the Kings of Israel (8:18) and Baalism became a cult in the land especially within the royal family.

In case we become too alarmed at this we are given an assuring word that Baalism, at this stage of its history, was to be given no chance finally to take over Judah. God was still determined that nothing would ever make him forget his pledge to David about his royal house (8:19). We need to be given this assurance, for we are soon to read that the whole house of David was almost wiped out. Jehoram of Judah, we are told, had a short reign marked by defeat at the hands of the King of Edom. After his death his son Ahaziah formed a close friendship with Jehoram (or 'Joram') King of Israel of whom we have already read so much.

With the beginning of the reign of this young King in Judah we have come almost to the point in time when Elisha commissioned Hazael to his life-work. The latter had lost no time before he went into action in a war to retake Ramoth of Gilead from Israel. Jehoram (here called 'Joram') was wounded, and retired from the field of battle to Jezreel where Ahaziah of Judah came to see him. Jehoram soon recovered from his wounds but delayed coming back to the battlefield, a delay which could be put down to the pleasant time he was having in the company of a fellow king.

Among the troops on the field at Ramoth there was a group of generals, most of them enemies of Baalism, and restless over the conduct of their King. They were possibly alarmed at the spread of Baal religion also in Judah. It irked them that their King had dallied so long in the comfort of his palace at Jezreel. Among them, Elisha knew, was Jehu, full of burning ardour to maintain the faith of his fathers, ruthless enough to stoop to any kind of deceit, ambitious to found a new dynasty and waiting for an opportunity to show his mettle. 'A blood thirsty man' is how Ellul describes him, 'at home in massacres, whose temperament corresponds with what is required of him'.

It must have seemed to Elisha when he heard of this staff convention, and tried to guage their feelings, that God had arranged exactly this meeting to be the occasion for the anointing of Jehu. Possibly he did not also realise that in bringing the two foolish kings together to be the first victims of Jehu's purge he was also opening up the way for an early and swift demonstration of what Jehu was later proudly to call 'my zeal for the Lord'.

The Anointing

Even though the circumstances were propitious and Jehu himself so ready to be encouraged, Elisha, after his experience before Hazael, found himself shrinking from being brought into direct involvement in the act he knew would have to be done. We can imagine the questions he raised with himself, as he thought it out: how could a man like Jehu, in the task he was to be given, ever reflect in his dealings with his people the image of patient, forgiving sovereign justice that a true King of Israel was meant to show to his people? What kind of reputation would the Lord have after this man was set free to work his will? He must have pled with God to be spared a repetition of the experience he had had with Hazael. God seems to have appreciated his protest and allowed him to send a substitute. A young man from the company of the prophets was selected. He was carefully briefed: nothing more was to be said than '*I anoint you King*'. He was then to '*flee*' and the instruction '*do not linger*' was added to emphasise that there had to be no fraternization or conversation of any kind.

The conversation that took place at the end of the affair gives us a glimpse of the amused disdain with which such prophets were viewed by both Jehu and his fellow officers: '*Why did that madman come to you?*', they asked Jehu, '*You know the sort and how they babble*' was his reply (9:11). That was the public conversation, but in private apart from them Jehu was thrilled to know that his ambition had divine sanction.

We are meant to notice how the young prophet disobeyed Elisha's careful instructions to say nothing and to flee immediately. His zeal made him give Jehu a detailed description of things which he believed from prophetic tradition had to be carried out. It was he and not Elisha who was responsible for telling him that he was to shed much blood, that he was to kill every member of the former household of Ahab and that he was to be swift and ruthless in his treatment of Jezebel. Was he, in doing so, making himself partly responsible for some of the fearful excesses which were to be perpetrated by the newly anointed King, and are we not meant at the prime event of Elisha's life to admire him all the more for his foresight and caution?

Notes

On the Date of the Shunammite's Return
The first incident related in this section of the narrative seems obviously to belong to a late period in Elisha's very long life. It is narrated here by the editor as a reminder of the immense popularity Elisha actually attained even before he undertook, as he is here about to do, the two important tasks which God had originally appointed him to carry out. After these two anointings he is to enter his long period of almost complete retirement and the record of his doings here referred to was almost complete. The king referred to here was most likely Jehoash.

On Elisha's Reluctant Obedience

To help us more fully to understand Elisha's reluctance in this chapter, it is worth while keeping in mind what Hazael did as the result of being made King of Aram. He skilfully murdered his king, and immediately launched an attack on Ramoth of Gilead in which Jehoram of Israel was wounded (2 Kings 8:28–29, 9:14–15). After being involved in an exhausting war with Assyria, he returned to harass Israel again, robbing Jehu of his lands east of Jordan ('threshing Gilead with threshing sledges of iron' — Amos 1:3, cf. 2 Kings 10:13–22). Jehu's successor Jehoahaz was oppressed by him throughout his whole reign, and at one point was left with 'not more than fifty horsemen, ten chariots, and ten thousand footmen' (2 Kings 13:22). He invaded Judah on a southern expedition to Gath, threatening Jerusalem and extracting a heavy tribute from the temple treasury from the terrified king Joash.

No doubt Elisha believed that God would be in control of those to whom he submitted his people for punishment in this way, and he believed that God would judge Hazael even for the wickedness involved in his service. Like Jeremiah, as we have pointed out, he could not overcome his horror at the prospect of what was to happen, and it is noticeable that God in no way rebuked him. Though Hazael's career lasted long, Elisha out-lived him, and on his death-bed he was able to express his hatred for the cruelty of the Aramean armies in the oracle he uttered to Joash (cf. II Kings 13:18–19).

We need not attach much significance to his appointing a deputy to anoint Jehu. It was Elijah who had been originally commissioned to this task. This anointing involves a whole set of new considerations and problems which will be discussed in the next chapter.

Points for Further Thought and Discussion

Think of how inspiring it can be for ourselves and those around us to have circulated and to read the lives and achievements of great Christian leaders. Do we give this a sufficient place in Christian education? Should we, more often than we do, thank God 'for all the saints, who from their labours rest'?

Here we have another example of the belief, held throughout the Bible, that the utterance of a Word of God, given to a prophet can have a decisive influence on human history as it brings about what is promised (cf. notes on p. 12 and p. 46). Reformed Church leaders like John Calvin and John Knox strongly believed that the preaching of the Word of God as it took place in the Church was bound to have a decisive effect on those who heard, and their social environment. Do you think such a claim and hope is relevant today?

We are reminded here that harsh things have sometimes to be done on earth if God's will is to be done. Moreover those involved in doing God's will have sometimes to steel their hearts in the tasks in which they are involved. Can we find ourselves today, as Elisha in his day, having to consent to, or co-operate in, decisions or actions, within Church or society, which go against the grain?

We have suggested that Elisha was given a quite unique gift of insight into the motive and character of another in his encounter with Hazael (like that of Peter in Acts 5:1–4) while we ourselves may be forced at times within the community life of the Church to make judgments on the outward behaviour or expressed opinions of another person, are we ever able, or ever meant, even to try to make deeper judgments about their inner motives or character? Read e.g. 1 Sam. 16:7, Jer. 17:9–10, and 1 Cor. 13:7 where we are urged to avoid being suspicious.

Do we ourselves, like Elisha, have on occasion to accept as our allies in the work of the Church, or to side with people and powers of whose motives and integrity we are not always certain? Like the prophet we have to accept their co-operation without fraternizing with them. What is your opinion of e.g. the blessing of a battleship by the Church?

CHAPTER X

JEHU

2 Kings 9:14–10:36

The Narrative

Without any pause to evaluate what is being done, we are told, with considerable detail and one after another, of the doings of Jehu, and the methods he used to destroy Baalism both within Israel and, as far as he could, also in Judah. We read of the assassination of the two kings, then of Jezebel, then of all that was left of the house of Ahab in the provinces, then of the princes of Judah, and finally of the great massacre in Samaria. During the last episode we are told of how he gained the co-operation of Jehonadab the son of Rechab. The account ends with a note on the modified approval of God for his service, on his failure entirely to serve God, and on the harassment he suffered by Hazael, King of Aram.

The Task and the Calling

The ministry of both Elijah and Elisha had been marvellously effective. Elijah, at Carmel, had decisively proved, as only Moses before him had done, that the Lord alone was the God who reigned on this earth, and that he demanded his people's absolute loyalty. In the work and witness of Elisha, ample signs of God's uniqueness, faithfulness and mercy had followed. After a whole generation of patient and convincing witness through the prophets, however, there were still many in Israel who had closed their minds, called the truth a lie and held on to Baal. The word God had spoken through Elijah could not have accomplished its purpose unless this continuing opposition was dealt with. When Edmund Burke was asked if he was afraid of the day of judgment, he replied, 'I would be more afraid of a day of no judgment'. The Lord God of Israel would not have been the powerful and loving God, true to his Word and faithful in his love if at this point in Israel's history, there had been no such day. His name for righteousness and truth had to be vindicated in face of the persistent arrogance of those who had defied him.

The God of the Bible, moreover, is never impassionate in his love. It is always a deeply-felt emotion, burning ardently to give itself expression, seeking to save and win those to whom it goes out. Likewise in seeking to establish and communicate his righteousness, God is always zealous. He does not go into action as a cold and calculating arbiter untouched by the nature of the offences that have been committed against him, or unconcerned about the fate and the destiny of those who stand before him. Always he is personally and fully involved. Holy Scripture speaks of him as a 'jealous God'. 'That is to say', says Ellul, 'he loves to such a degree that he cannot bear it that his creatures should not finally be saved. He cannot bear it that man should turn to someone other than himself.'

Throughout the history of Israel therefore, where God enlisted leaders or prophets into his service, they, too, became passionate in his service. They found themselves obeying his will not simply because they wanted to render dutiful obedience under his instructions, but because at the same time they found themselves inspired to do so. They were inwardly stirred up by the same zeal for the task as had already been possessed by God himself. They shared with God himself the same living passion for the work they were to do in his name. Moses, for example, when he arrived in the camp of Israel after his sojourn with God on the mountain, and saw the promiscuous dancing and the idolatry, did not need to be told by God how to act, or what to do. He found himself wholly possessed by the same burning wrath as he had already encountered in God on the mountain, and he simply expressed and reflected it in the punishment he meted out to the offenders (Exod. 32:19ff.). When Elijah, at Horeb, tried to explain to God what had happened to him at Carmel, he described himself as having been there caught up with a 'zeal of the Lord of hosts' that it was quite beyond his natural power to sustain (1 Kings 19:10, 14), and we have no doubt that Elisha, too, in his experience at the translation of Elijah (cf. 2 Kings 2:12-14) found himself so possessed.

Though Jehu was a layman, nevertheless we find that from the moment of his call to purge the remnants of Baalism for ever from Israel, he too found himself possessed by a passion in his heart driving him to the action he was to take. He interpreted this burning concern as divinely kindled by God himself. Moreover he held before his mind the examples of zeal for the Lord set by his forerunners in the faith like Moses, Samuel and Elijah and ranked himself along with them.

It is true that very soon after he began his mission, he allowed his vision to become to some extent obscure, and his aim corrupted. Nevertheless, if we are fully to understand this story, and God's immediate acceptance of his service, we must assume that such ideals were important to him when he set out on his career.

The Point of Failure

Immediately we begin reading the account before us of Jehu's attempt to give expression to God's abhorrence of Baalism, in his brilliantly successful campaign, we find ourselves disturbed by questions about the value of the service he was seeking to give, and the integrity of the man himself.

It is true that to obtain his throne, he had to execute Jehoram whom he encountered near the spot where Naboth had been murdered. Yet we have to ask ourselves if there was any need for him to have the dead body, without any respect, simply thrown like a bag of rubbish on the spot where the death had been prophesied to happen. Moreover, at the same time, without any call to do so, was there any need to pursue the hapless young King of Judah so ruthlessly to his death? And in murdering Jezebel, did he really need to act as if he were thoroughly enjoying himself? (9:1-37).

He certainly had a remit to slay the sons of Ahab. Yet the hypocritical cunning with which he set about the task heightens the revulsion we already feel against him. These princes, all possible rivals to the throne of Israel were located in many different provinces. They were under the supervision and protection of the governors and elders of each area. Jehu's sudden murder of the King had left the local governors no time to consult and weigh up their common situation. He seized the initiative and wrote to each separately. He suggested that each governor nominate from among those sons of Ahab around him a suitable candidate for the kingship. Both the dispatch and the tone of the letter were a challenge to them not to be foolish enough to put an obstacle in Jehu's own way, and each governor felt constrained to make no nomination leaving the election of the future king in the usurper's hands. His next move in the cat and mouse game he was playing with them, was to assume complete authority, and to send a second message which was designedly ambiguous. Each was ordered to '*take the heads of your master's sons*' and meet him at Jezreel the next day! The message could have been read: 'count their number and bring a record of them to me!' Or it could have meant: 'decapitate them'! Jehu had already aroused so much terror by his ways and actions that the governors universally interpreted it in the latter way. The climax was a needlessly cynical display of self-righteousness on Jehu's part. The seventy heads were heaped in two piles for public exhibition overnight, and the new king in his speech the next day exonerated himself from all responsibility. He had not himself devised such a slaughter! Certainly, he admitted, he had killed Jehoram, but he himself had no responsibility for bringing about this carnage! Surely the Lord was now vindicating his own completely established right to the throne! (10:1–11).

As we read on, we suspect that his concern for his public reputation at this stage in his career was part of his scheme to win popular support for the final mass killing of the Baal devotees, trapped in their temple by blatant deceit and given no chance of escape or repentance (10:18–24).

Before this final act of terror, we read of the completely unprovoked slaying of the seventy princes of Judah, a deed entirely beyond any remit he had had from God. By now, the more blood he shed, the more he appears to have wanted to shed. He seems to have believed that with providence on his side so magnificently, he might eventually succeed to the throne of Judah as well as to that of Israel (10:12–14).

Some commentators uncritically defend Jehu, and God's use of him. They argue that the situation then prevailing in Israel presented such extreme and exceptional difficulties that, in order to meet it, God had no alternative than to allow himself to be served by this kind of man with his crude brutality. Gentler actions by milder characters could not have made the necessary impact! It can indeed be argued that even deceit and cunning had to be used against an enemy who understood and practised no other way!

We have to admit that God at times, in order to vindicate his name, to express his righteous anger, and thus to fulfil his purposes, had to be devastatingly severe in the judgments with which he visited his people. He had to allow himself to become involved in what was to him a 'strange' or 'alien' work (cf. Isa. 28:21). The sword, here in Israel, had to be used, and the task given to Jehu was abhorrent.

What offends us so greatly about Jehu, however, is that he did not find anything strange or alien in the work he had to do and showed not a trace of reluctance in doing it. Here we are given the impression of a man who seems to be without compunction or compassion, whose aim appears at times to be, not to restore righteousness but to establish a reign of terror.

When Moses at times was given the same kind of negative work, he often found the task hateful to himself, showed hesitation in carrying it through, and prayed to God to spare the people the suffering and shame with which they were being inflicted. There is not a trace of such feelings in Jehu. This was his great fault and, as we shall see, it undoubtedly spoiled the full effectiveness of the witness he was raised up by God to give.

Yet God Sees and Accepts!

Frank though this writer's account is of Jehu's faults, he has no hesitation at the same time, in underlining also God's acceptance of what Jehu accomplished: '*You have done well in carrying out what I consider right.*' He records that Jehu was made the founder of a long dynasty: '*Your sons of the fourth generation shall sit on the throne*' (10:30). His record of this dynasty will, as we shall see, reveal it to have great potential for good (cf. pp. 136ff.). Jehu is here blamed by God only because like all other kings of Israel, he did not turn from '*the sins of Jeroboam*' (10:31). Before we make any final judgment on him, therefore, we are called on to regard him as a man genuinely seeking to serve God even while he was tragically mistaken in the action he took, and to appreciate his immediate achievement in cleansing Israel, and the zeal with which he put his heart into everything he did.

We are certainly not being called here to become uncritical. 'God is not mocked, for you reap whatever you sow' (Gal. 6:7). Jehu certainly too easily became a national hero within the dynasty he set up in Israel. His callous cruelties and debased trickery became a fondly remembered aspect of the national tradition which too many others in the succeeding generations were tempted to follow (cf. pp. 142, 149) and in the fourth generation of his dynasty there came on Israel the final judgment of God pronounced beforehand by the prophet Hosea: 'In a little while I will punish the house of Jehu for the blood of Jezreel, and I will put an end to the Kingdom of the house of Israel' (Hosea 1:4).

At this moment in the history, however, we have to acknowledge that God found in Jehu's service what was then 'acceptable' in his sight (cf. Ps. 19:14 A.V.). Jehu himself may have been quite unaware that he was inserting a streak of harsh cruelty into his national tradition, and God may have hoped that his successors on the throne would renounce wholly their father's excesses and establish better ways among their people. Jehu is therefore held out here to us as an example as well as a warning. It is brought home to us here, as in other parts of Holy Scripture that 'the Lord does not see as mortals see; they look on the outward appearance, but the Lord looks on the heart' (1 Sam. 16:7). Though in the outward expression of Jehu's zeal (i.e. in its 'outward appearance') there was so much that was distorted, ugly and uncontrolled, nevertheless the motive that inspired his behaviour, deep down in the heart, was genuine. In spite of superficially corrupting elements which entered so damagingly into his behaviour and so tragically into his example, yet the dominating passion in his life had been to express and reflect the passion for God's righteousness with which he had felt himself gripped when his call had come to destroy evil.

This may be the reason why '*Jehonadab the son of Rehab*' is brought so prominently into the story here, to stand as an approving human witness to the worth of Jehu's achievement in the service of God. Jehonadab's father Rechab had achieved fame in his day by renouncing some of the customs of the settled world of his day. Jehonadab and his family eventually won a good and lasting reputation in the history of Israel (see note). On many aspects of life he had very different ideas and ideals than those of Jehu. But Jehu respected him and felt his support could help his cause. Therefore as he was passing him on the roadside he drew up his chariot and in a very dramatic fashion gave him the challenge: '*Is your heart as true to mine as mine is to yours?*' Jehonadab had already made his decision and spontaneously took the offered hand and rode on with him. We are meant to note the overcoming of all prejudice between two men who both recognised the urgency for mutual support in the name of the Lord in face of the devilish opposition they felt themselves up against. Jehu was certainly not Jehonadab's 'type', but he recognised that God was using him. In this simple little incident there may be a warning for some of us to heed. If we ourselves had been involved we would have been inclined to hold ourselves aloof from the kind of person we perceived Jehu to be — not our type! Thus we can both narrow down our sphere of influence, and deprive ourselves, and our Church, too, from enrichment, strength and enthusiasm. We must not be too ready to act on the assumption that the outward appearance reveals what is in the heart.

Most importantly, the story of Jehu stands before us here as a reminder of how God desires wholeheartedness in his service. There is a striking incident in the Book of Numbers which was possibly in Jehu's mind when he set out on his revolutionary career in the service of God. It took place at a critical point in the travels of Israel through the wilderness when their whole future was in doubt. Their men were incurring God's anger by freely entering sexual relations with foreign women. A plague struck them and many were perishing. Phinehas, one of Aaron's grandsons happened to see a man of Israel publicly and defiantly taking a Midianite woman into his tent. In burning indignation, immediately and spontaneously he took a spear, advanced, entered the tent and thrust it into the two of them, the whole congregation witnessing. It is affirmed that God was thrilled with what he saw done by Phinehas. He stopped the plague. He told Moses that he had been on the point of consuming Israel because no one except himself seemed to be jealous for his name. But now Phinehas' action had changed the whole human situation as he saw it. God is said to have been so thrilled by this vindication of his holiness that he made a 'covenant of peace' for Phinehas and his descendants 'because he was zealous for his God, and made atonement for the Israelites' (Nu. 25:6–13, see note). When God sees true zeal for his glory and his name burning in a human heart, he sees a reflection within human life of his own jealousy for his purposes and his love.

We are here at the heart of the New Testament as well as of the Old. Here was what Jesus himself offered to God on our behalf —a heart burning continually with pure zeal for his glory and kingdom, and ready to be consumed wholly in the sacrifice that a life so lived would demand (cf. Ps. 69:9, John 2:17). And does he not seek to create in us continually the same burning hearts (cf. Luke 24: 32) so that we too will have our consciences delivered from all 'dead works' to give him living service (Heb. 9:14)? 'No heart is pure that is not passionate' said John Seeley in a once famous book on the Gospels, 'no virtue is safe that is not enthusiastic'.

True Zeal and its Vulnerability

We have seen that Jehu's zeal, though it was acceptable to God, was nevertheless flawed because his mind was too narrowly focussed on executing the judgment of God, in forgetfulness of his need also to witness to his care and compassion for the individual. Jacques Ellul rightly points out how fixedly his mind was taken over by the desire to fulfil the details of the one prophecy which he happened to hear Elijah pronounce on Ahab, and which was repeated to him by the over-zealous young prophet sent to him by Elisha (cf. 1 Kings 21:21–24, 2 Kings

9:7-10). It involved the destruction of Jezebel with her 'whoredoms and sorceries' and the annihilation of the house of Ahab (cf. 9:21ff.). We can accuse him of concentrating on this word of God, and of forgetting the nature of the God who spoke it. We can note, moreover, the prominence of his own self-consciousness in describing the passion of his heart to Jehonadab: '*Come with me, and see my zeal for the Lord*' (10:16). Our suspicion is that he has become more concerned simply to be zealous in his own chosen way rather than to remain wholly under God's inspiration and direction. We find ourselves asking if he has begun to cut himself loose and to take over from God? We cannot doubt that when God first called him to his task, and kindled his enthusiasm for it, he did everything he could to lift Jehu's mind above all narrowing restrictions of thought about his mission. God then must have reminded Jehu that he loved mercy and had compassion even on those he chastised. But Jehu gave neither time nor room for such a word to take root in his mind. This means that his zeal became what we can call 'eccentric' and dangerous.

Too often in the history of the Church it has happened that, in their zeal to serve God, Christian people have followed the example of Jehu, concentrated all their energy on upholding only one too narrow aspect of the faith, and as a result have given a distorted witness to the truth. There are aspects of the whole message of the life, cross and resurrection of Jesus which offend the human mind — especially when it wounds our human pride and condemns our accepted human customs. We are apt, in our desire to make it more comfortable to ourselves and more popular to others to select only those aspects of it which fit most comfortably into our predilections. Today, for example, the danger often is that we take our whole Gospel from the parable of the Prodigal Son forgetting the need for atonement, stressing how freely he loves us, and forgetting entirely that he hates and judges sin. We have to remember always that he reveals himself in Christ as both merciful *and* righteous, as both loving *and* holy. The Old Testament demonstrates time and again his holy wrath against sin and his holy love for sinners (cf. Isa. 45:21). The New Testament tells us that his righteousness as well as his love is revealed in the sacrifice of the cross (cf. Rom. 3:25–26).

We are only safe in the exercise of such zeal as Jehu showed, when it is directed to the glory of God alone and arises out of love to him. Zeal in any sphere of life is always vulnerable, for we are always in danger of misdirecting it. In secular life, for instance, concentrating too much of our energy and devotion on one particular aspect of the challenge life brings to us, at the expense of, and sometimes to the neglect of, other equally important (or even more important!) aspects, can often be damaging. In a recent BBC interview an ardent well-known animal rights' campaigner admitted that she had become so fanatical for the cause of animal welfare that she had come to despise ordinary humankind, and that her marriage had broken up as a result. It would be foolish for a general conducting a war and facing an enemy whose forces were extended over a wide front, to concentrate too many of his own limited resources on one narrow sector. In Church life, too, it can happen that, for example, we concentrate our energy and devotion so absorbingly on upholding purity and exactness in the sphere of Church doctrine, that we tend to neglect the call to evangelise and serve people, and we can become so zealous for one narrow aspect of morality that we neglect other important issues. It was this kind of fault about which Jesus was warning us when he said 'these things ought ye to have done, and not to leave the other undone' (Matt. 23:23 A.V.). We must remember that the zeal of the Pharisees for their false interpretation of the law became a cloak behind which, according to Jesus, they hid their deep insincerity of heart.

Notes

On God's Zeal in Love and Justice
If we are to do justice to the Biblical witness to the nature of God, we have to speak of both his love and justice, of his mercy and wrath in their togetherness. God feels both wholeheartedly and passionately, and he seeks to give expression to both aspects of his nature in the way he works out his providence and the history of salvation. At times he will conceal and hold back his wrath in order clearly to proclaim his love. At times the reverse will take place. 'He hides himself from us,' says Isaiah 'with

overflowing wrath', yet at the same time he is seeking to gather ourselves to him with 'great compassion' (cf. Isa. 54:7–8). He is both together, 'a just God and a Saviour' (Isa. 45:21). The New Testament, of course, underlines his love, but never forgets that the God who loves us is a 'consuming fire' (Heb. 12:29) into whose hands it is a 'fearful thing' to fall (Heb. 10:31). The Cross is the true and final expression of both his just work and his overflowing mercy (Rom. 3:25–26). Here we see, as Vischer put it, 'the holy love of his wrath and the holy wrath of his love'.

Hosea who was led to utter God's final judgment on Jehu spoke time and again invitingly of God's love (11:19, 14:1–9) and warned of the imminent threat of his justice (1:4, 8:1–14, 7:4–7), and in a memorable passage he gives vivid expression to a tension which believes God to feel between them as his heart (11:8–9).

It is in this context of revelation that we are to understand why Hosea could condemn Jehu so severely. He must have approved that Jehu had been deeply concerned to give expression to God's burning hatred of Baalism. There was special need at that time for such a witness. God had accepted and recorded this service. But judgment had eventually to be passed on the distortion of the image of God that had marred his effort, especially in view of the long-term effects of his example to posterity, the subtle and prevailing evil influence of that example on the common people in the dynasty which he founded.

The Rechabites

We learn about the Rechabites from an incident in the Book of Jeremiah as a protest against the whole way of life which the Hebrews had to adopt when they became a settled farming community in Canaan after their wilderness wanderings, Jonadab, the son of Rechab, commanded his descendants not to build houses or adopt settled agricultural practices. They were to live in tents and not to plant vineyards or to drink wine. During the siege of Jerusalem by Nebuchadnezzar, the Rechabites around the city were forced to take refuge within its walls, and Jeremiah commended them for being so faithful to their vows and convictions in contrast to the citizens of

Jerusalem who were proving their faithlessness and disobedience to God (Jer. 35:8-10). There is a suggestion in 1 Chron. 2:55 that the original inspiration for their way of life may here come from the Kenites who associated with Moses in the wilderness (cf. Judges 4:11-12).

Points for Further Thought and Discussion

Though Jehu was not a prophet and his task as soldier and king in the service of God involved so much the use of force, he was no less solemnly anointed by God for his task in life than was Elijah. He is to be judged by God as to how he did it. Read Romans 13:1–5 where Paul too regards rulers as instituted by God, and his servants 'to execute wrath'. Do we, and those in authority today take this seriously enough, and would it make a difference if we did?

We cannot doubt that Jehu was well-intentioned, yet at the same time he was in some measure also self-deluded. Is this a common fault today, and a point on which we should examine ourselves?

Read Eph. 5:11, and its context. Are there depraved and at times criminal social practices around us today of the kind which led Jehu into his ardent crusade against Baalism? Are we ourselves in our witness to the truth giving adequate expression in our words and attitude to an abhorrence of such practices?

Jehu damaged God's reputation among his people, nation and possibly abroad. God who cared deeply for the honour of his name, even though he rewarded Jehu, must have felt the hurt. 'In his zeal for God,' says Ellul, 'it is God himself whom Jehu strikes.' Can you think of how what we do, often with zeal, within the Church, (and in our personal lives too) also does him hurt today?

Think of other instances than those already given in which zeal to respond to one aspect of human need tends to blind us and others to even more urgent needs, of how over emphasis on a side-issue leads to neglect of main issues, both in secular and church life. Are we ourselves perhaps directly involved?

CHAPTER XI

JUDAH — FROM ATHALIAH TO JOASH
2 Kings 11:1–12:21

The Narrative

Athaliah seizing her opportunity to usurp the throne of Judah, planned to kill all possible rival claimants including the dead king's children. Unknown to her Jehosheba stole the infant Joash, the true heir, from the palace, and for six years, in conspiracy with her husband the high priest Jehonadab, reared him in the temple, finally arranging to have him at the age of six anointed and crowned king in a dramatic counter-revolution, when Athaliah was assassinated. The reign of Joash was marked especially by the renovation of the temple buildings and a lastingly effective re-organisation of its financial support. It was positive and healthy as long as he remained under the influence of Jehonadab, but when the latter died, he tragically began to go astray.

(Note: Joash, as the account develops, is often referred to as 'Jehoash'.)

Athaliah Triumphant

From everything we are told about Jehu in the previous chapters we have been given the impression that, even as he began his campaign, he had his eye on the throne of Judah as well as on that of Israel. The idea of such an achievement could have come to his mind immediately he saw the easy opportunity before him of killing its king, Ahaziah, along with Jehoram,

his own king. Believing himself to be under the inspiration
and guidance of God, he may have read this opportunity as a
clear call to this further divine mission. The same ambition
motivated his ruthless slaughter of the seventy princes of Judah
when they fell into his hand. The ease with which this was
accomplished made him feel he could now with support from
the people bring about in Judah an anti-Baal revolution
corresponding to that in Israel, and, of course, the throne of
Judah, too, would be his.

At the very moment when he had completed the rout of
Baalism in his own kingdom, however, and was ready for action
in Judah, he found himself thwarted by Hazael, king of Aram.
The very man God had raised up to side with him in putting
Baal worshippers to the sword (cf. 1 Kings 19:17) began to
attack his territory and involved him in an exhausting and
expensive war. When God is using rogues and brutes to do his
will, he is marvellously able to limit their power and success by
matching them against each other.

Obviously, God had his own plans for dealing with Baalism
in Judah, and he allowed the throne to be taken over by
Athaliah, the mother of the king Jehu had murdered. We can
only speculate on what prompted her to take this action. Her
son Ahaziah had been a weak person, who had allowed his
mother not only to become the dominant figure in a large
royal family, but also to promote the service of Baal throughout
the land. Jehu by his slaughter of the family which she had so
wholly dominated, had destroyed her power base and left her
in a weak and isolated position in a largely alien community.
But she had showed the same resilience as had characterised
her mother Jezebel after Carmel. Bishop Hall thinks that it
was in an effort to spite Jehu that she seized the throne herself.
We can think of her, rather, as acting out of an implacable
determination to defy the God of Israel even though she must
have known in her heart that ultimately she would be beaten.
In her desperate bid to hold on to power she had to plan the
massacre of '*all the royal family*' (11:1). She did everything with
serene self-righteous dignity and with a feeling that she was
acting heroically in the service of the lord Baal. We are appalled
by her massacre of the innocents (see note). Could even Herod
have stooped to the cold-blooded murder of his own

grandchildren? Her achievement was remarkable. No other woman had reigned on the throne she seized, and having begun in such a repulsive way, with such frail support, it is a proof of her extraordinary ability and skill that she was able to keep her throne for six years. Racine, the great French dramatist was so fascinated by the situation she faced, and the way she took it, that he made her the heroine of a marvellously worked out tragedy, which inspired Handel to write one of his great oratorios.

As we follow through the drama of her life we will discover that the way she took in her arrogance and pride proved in the end to be self-destructive. The infant king whom she willed to destroy eventually proved himself to be the kind of person who allowed his beliefs and his way of life to be too easily determined by those who were in a position of influence around him. If Athaliah had simply allowed him to grow up under her tutelage she could in the long run have retained her power and devastating influence in the kingdom of Judah as long as she herself lived. As it was, she sealed her own much speedier doom in the decision she made.

Jehosheba and Jehonadab

Athaliah's attempt to kill the royal prince was thwarted by the devotion, imagination and initiative of a young woman open to godly concern about what was happening in the world around her, and ready to ask herself if there was something she was meant to do about it. No divine instructions came to Jehosheba direct from heaven. She possibly found her inspiration and example in the story of Moses; hidden by his mother and saved from an untimely death because God had a great destiny for him. She herself must have felt impelled and strengthened in the action she took by the promise about the house of David which must have been in circulation then in some form: 'His line shall continue for ever, and his throne endure before me like the sun' (Ps. 89:36 N.I.V.). Her faith made her remarkably free from fear 'By faith Moses was hidden by his parents for three months after his birth... for they were not afraid' (Heb. 11:23). So it was with Jehosheba. One false step and her life was at stake. God gave her the nerve she needed.

Much more than one simple act of baby-snatching is implied in the brief intimation that she '*stole him away*' when he was '*about to be killed*' (11:2). Some of the older commentators, asked not only how the theft was carried out, but how she managed to dupe Athahiah (who must have carefully supervised the whole affair) by substituting a dead child from elsewhere among the corpses which the usurper must have wanted at least to count! There are many other features of the story that give us food for thought at this point. It is significant that here at this stage in the turmoil of human history God allowed the fulfilment of his promises to David to depend on the fate of an infant about to be murdered! It is even more significant that, as elsewhere in Holy Scripture, God makes the future of his severely threatened kingdom to depend not on the military prowess of a saviour like Jehu, or even on the preaching of an impressive Elijah, but on the dedicated self-offering of a young woman, willing to say 'Here am I, servant of the Lord'! (Luke 1:38). Time and again God chooses what is weak in the world to shame the strong (1 Cor. 1:27). Here, he overcomes Satanic power with gentleness and pity, evil with good.

Of course, as along with Mary there was Joseph, so along with Jehosheba there was Jehonadab. She could not even have conceived the plan without relying on his support. The Book of Chronicles after the notice of his death at the age of a hundred and thirty years, ranks him among the great. 'They buried him in the city of David among the kings, because he had done good in Israel, and for God and his house' (2 Chron. 24:15–16). Again here we would like to have more details, for example, of how he managed to ward off the frequent intrusions into the temple by the children of 'that wicked woman' Athaliah (cf. 2 Chron. 24:7). How did he manage to keep the presence of the child in the temple a complete secret till he could be safely presented to the people? He could have finally achieved such long-time secrecy only by a sheer miracle of God's providential oversight in the temple affairs. The story, without directly saying it, brings us a promise from God, that when his service involves wisdom, enduring patience and diplomatic skill on our part over against even the Satanic cunning of an Athaliah, we will not lack what we need.

Kindled Hope and Renewed Vision

Even as the time approached to bring about the revolution, Athaliah was seen by the conspirators to be in an extremely powerful position — able to cause reaction, strife and danger to the young king. Success seemed to depend on her being taken completely by surprise. Jehonadab's control of the situation in the kingdom comes out magnificently as the whole affair reaches its climax. They chose the exact moment when the loyal element of the temple guard normally split up, were brought together to provide enough protection for the prince from a possible opposition from the palace, and marvellously, too, the secret of what was to happen was kept. The scene is impressively described: '*The guards stood, every man with his weapons in his hand, from the south side of the house to the north side of the house, around the altar and the house, to guard the king on every side. Then he brought out the king's son, put the crown on him and gave him the covenant; they proclaimed him king and anointed him; they clapped their hands and shouted, "Long live the king"*' (11:11–12).

The crown was to be the most prominent part of the official wear of the youngster, designed to give him an aura of external majesty and to add to the 'beauty' of his person (cf. Isa. 62:3, Jer. 13:18). The anointing was much more significant. It was a sign that God had chosen him for this divinely appointed office, set him apart from all others to be given unique respect and honour, and that God would protect him and bestow on him all the gifts of wisdom and leadership necessary for the work to which he was called. The giving of the 'covenant' may have been, as Wiseman suggests, 'a copy of the ten commandments and the mosaic covenant, especially the regulations regarding the obligations of kingship' (Deut. 17:14–20; 1 Sam 10:17–25).

It was a great moment in their national life when they proclaimed him king. 'Hardly could the multitude contain itself from shouting out too soon', writes Bishop Hall. 'One sees in his countenance the features of his father, Ahaziah, another of his grandfather Jehoram, some the likeness and fashion of Jehoshaphat. All find in his face the natural impressions of majesty, and read in it the hopes, yes, the prophecies of future happiness.' It was no doubt one of these moments when the vision of their great messianic future as the people of God again possessed the minds of the far-seeing and faithful among them: the same kind of vision as possessed their prophets when at even more depressing times they uttered their great prophecies about that future. This particular moment would have been a perfect occasion for words like those of Psalm 126 to express what they felt:

'When the Lord restored the fortunes of Zion,
    We were like those who dream.
Then our mouth was filled with laughter,
    and our tongue with shouts of joy.'

Athaliah, taken completely by surprise, was too shocked even to think of any counter-movement. She made only a pathetically weak protest against what was to her, base '*treason*', and yielded to her inevitable death with the same personal dignity as her mother Jezebel had done. The writer does not tell us that her body was buried, simply that she was '*killed with the sword*' and that '*the city was quiet*' (11:20). No one mourned for her. God had dealt a more effective final blow to Baalism in Judah than even Jehu could have done.

It was under these circumstances that '*Jehoiada made a covenant between the Lord and the king and people, that they should be the Lord's people*' (11:17).

Joash — the Achievement

We are now told that the most significant achievements of Joash during his forty years' reign were the restoration of the temple buildings, and the reorganisation of its finances. The structure had suffered serious neglect, and some of it had been destroyed during the Athaliah regime. While the urgent repairs were being met, the young king discovered that money meant for the fabric fund was too easily mixed up with that for priestly support. The people themselves were naturally reluctant to give of their gifts while there was uncertainty about its ultimate use. Hitherto, too much of the temple finance had depended on the generosity and goodwill of the reigning king — a source which had been too casual and had by now proved unstable. We are told with great detail that Joash therefore devised and set up a new system with a central collecting box, the contents of which were to be regularly counted and fairly distributed under careful supervision. This simple reform had the long-term effect of making the upkeep of the temple dependent on the givings of the people so that it would no longer be thought of as a royal chapel, but rather as a place belonging to the people of God. It brought in a greater openness in administration. We are given one small illustration of the immediate improvement. We are told that the priests in their zeal for the trivial embellishments of their trade were now prevented from using the precious gifts of the people 'to make silver cups, snuffers, tossing-bowls, trumpets, or any gold or silver vessels'. The money, instead, was paid to the workmen and used for repairs (12:13 N.E.B.).

The introduction of this new system of Church finance may seem to us today to be a very obvious and simple reform, but many things which we take for granted today took great skill and initiative on the part of those who pioneered them, and the writer is here paying his tribute to Joash, and to Jehonadab too, for enterprise and progressiveness. That Jesus watched the widow putting her money 'into the treasury' (Mark 12:41–42) is a reminder of the lasting nature of one aspect of the reform he pioneered.

All this is, no doubt, the achievement that the historian is referring to when he says that *'Jehoash did what was right in the sight of the Lord all his days, because the priest Jehoiada instructed him'* (12:2). Jehoiada has to be given credit for his personal influence, but the king himself is described as taking the initiative and responsibility for the reform and rebuilding. He was concerned, we can believe with much more than mere business routine. Obviously during his prime he never forgot how God gave his presence to his people and powerfully entered his own life on that day of his coronation and covenant. To him the temple was indeed the dwelling-place of the Lord. He believed with all his heart that the true well-being and prosperity of his people depended, above all else, on their being able to meet him there again and again both individually and in community. If such encounter with the living God himself, remembering his covenant, receiving his forgiving grace and marvellous self-revelation, could continue and become the basis of all their life together, their future as God's people, their safety among the nations, brotherhood and social justice among themselves, would be assured.

We are not meant, therefore, to feel in any way 'let down' when, immediately after his thrilling and dramatic account of the coronation of Joash we are told that the chief achievement of his long life was therefore in the realm of Church finance and building maintenance. Here is one of these places in Scripture where what can happen on one great temple occasion can determine the course of a lifetime (cf. Isa. 6:1ff.).

This apparently low-level account of long-term faithfulness in small every-day affairs is no less significant than a list of outstanding social diplomatic, or even military achievements would have been. The 'small things' we are sometimes tempted to despise (cf. Zech. 4:10) can be matters of infinite significance as God inserts them into the purposes he is slowly working out as year follows year.

Great days of vision are sometimes given to us by God to inspire us not to spectacular or unusual feats, but to get down to performing the ordinary tasks of life, with greater faithfulness and care for detail, than we have ever hitherto given. Immediately after his exultant climax to his chapter on the resurrection of Jesus in his first letter to the Corinthians, Paul felt it to be appropriate to descend quite abruptly to the routine and mundane. With the echo of his triumphant thanksgiving still in our ears, he reminds us about the need precisely *now* to be 'steadfast' in the ordinary work of the Church, and 'immoveable' in the face of every diversion, and without delay he turns to the details of finding an adequate method of collecting the money for the Church (1 Cor. 15:55–16:1).

Joash — the Final Tragedy and Shame

The historian in the Book of Kings, as if he wanted to preserve in our minds at least some of the credit (see note) which he has accorded to Joash for his years of faithful service to God, has deliberately emphasised only the tragic nature of his last days. He tells us that Jerusalem was seriously threatened by Hazael of Aram, and adds pathetically that the city had to be saved by almost exhausting all the temple treasures that it had been Joash's life-work and pride to conserve and build up. He tells us, without giving any reason for it, that there was a conspiracy against him, and he was murdered.

We have to turn to the Book of Chronicles to discover that his end was even more shameful than tragic. He evidently lost his vision of God, degenerated in character and listened to false counsel from the leaders who replaced Jehoiada. He set up idols and asherim. Signs of God's displeasure, and the protests of many unnamed prophets were unheeded. Finally Zechariah the high priest, the son of Jehoiada, rased his voice to proclaim to Joash that he would now be forsaken by God, 'King Joash did not remember the kindness that Jehoiada, Zechariah's father, had shown him', but had him 'stoned to death in the court of the house of the Lord' (2 Chron. 24:17–22). The chronicler tells us that it was a small Aramaean expeditionary force that defeated a large Judaean army. This defeat was a further sign of God's displeasure against Joash, who was wounded in the battle, and then murdured by his disaffected officials.

Having been reminded in the last chapter of the vulnerability of zeal we are now reminded of the vulnerability of a life overtaken by routine. For many of us, our service of Christ and the Church can begin with an experience similar to that of Joash in the temple — the vision, the call, the kindled emotion, the covenant are all there. But the memory even of such events can become so dim that we no longer grasp the reality of what is beyond the surface of things (cf. John 14:8–9). We no longer hear the living voice that once called us. We lose our sense of purpose. Even the conduct of the worship, the study of the word, the teaching and the preaching become a weight we have to carry instead of a continual source of inspiration. The last days of Joash remind us of the vision John Bunyan had of a road to hell from the gate of heaven. We have to note that Joash was the first king of Judah to come to a violent end.

Notes

On the Account of the Conspiracy against Athaliah etc.
The complicated nature of the account of the conspiracy against Athaliah, and the double account of her death, has led scholars to believe that it contains a combination of two distinct descriptions of one event. It is, further, pointed out that in the account of the event in Chronicles, Levites are the chief constituents of the kings' bodyguard, since 'Carites' would be regarded as unfitting within the sanctuary. Moreover there are differing accounts in Kings and Chronicles of the occurrence of, and happenings in, the war between Israel and Aram which led to the death of Joash (though, as McConville suggests, these may be accurate accounts of two different occasions). To unravel all this the student is advised to consult the standard commentaries.

On the Differing Biblical Assessments of Joash
McConville in his commentary on Chronicles is, from the point of view of that book, justifiably severe in his condemnation of, Joash's murderous response to love, which exposes apostasy in its most abominable form. We are reminded of Christ's condemnation of his infamy in Luke 11:49–51, and of the warning in Hebrews (6:4–6), that his behaviour is like that of 'crucifying again the Son of God'.

The entire Biblical account however inspires us to speculate on why the author of Kings felt justified in omitting the full account of Joash's last days. Could it have been that he believed the unfortunate king was himself overcome by a senility for which he had no personal responsibility (Alzheimer's disease?), or was it simply that he did not want his generous admiration for his marvellous early deliverance and achievement to become in any way overshadowed? The key verse is 'Joash did not remember the kindness that Jehoiada, Zechariah's father, had shown him (2 Chron. 24:22). If this was wilful, we have to accept the condemnation fully. If it was simply a very tragic aspect of his old age we can understand why the writer was anxious to cover over the shame of his behaviour.

We have to remember in our assessment of the man that his whole life was lived under the sign of God's grace. What would have become of him if he had been brought up in the court of his idolatrous father and his depraved mother?

Points for Further Thought and Discussion

As her life-situation developed around her, Jehosheba, perhaps suddenly, realised that God had placed her where she was as the key person to take the action on which the future and welfare of many others was to depend. Compare e.g. the situation of Esther (in Esther chapters 4–5) as the one person on whose action the future of her people depended. Is it not true that in a much smaller scale of life situations develop around us in home, place of work etc. where we too find ourselves as this key person who can take the action that can make all the difference, and blameable if we do not risk taking the action and perhaps speaking the word?

Think of the power of friendship especially of friendship made in Christ (cf. Gal. 6:2) and of the limits to what friendship can do for us (cf. Gal. 6:5). Am I open enough to the help a friendship can bring me, am I over dependent?

There seems to be a warning in this story that, after a dedicated life of service responding to the call of God a good beginning can come to a tragic end. The Old Testament shows us a God infinitely patient, everlasting in his love, however sinful Israel becomes. The New Testament tells us that we are in the hands of the same God who will never let us go or forsake us (cf. John 10:27–29) and yet there are warnings like Matt. 10:22 and Heb. 6:4–6. What do you think?

Here we have the example of a great occasion seized on to lead the people into fresh and solemn public vows that they should 'be the Lord's people'. It is suggested that such a momentary occasion of covenant vow-making had a lasting effect on the king and community. While we ourselves every Sunday should have a memorable occasion for vow-making, especially at the Lord's Table, is it also good practice in e.g. religious 'crusades' to re-create such unique public moments of re-dedication?

We are given the impression here that infinite care about details of the temple upkeep and administration of its finances were a genuine sign of Joash's piety and dedication to God. Are we sufficiently appreciative of the depth of personal dedication and commitment to Christ that time and again lies behind the regular routine of keeping our Church offices, buildings and finances in decent order today?

CHAPTER XII

THE DYNASTY OF JEHU
2 Kings 13:1–14:29

The Narrative

We are given here in the thirteenth chapter, brief accounts of the reigns of the first two kings to succeed Jehu on the throne of Israel, Jehoahaz and Joash (sometimes called Jehoash). It was during the reign of Joash that Elisha died and we are told of an incident at his death-bed when he was visited by the king seeking his help in the devastating war which Hazael, King of Aram, had continually waged against his country since the time of Jehu, his grandfather.

The fourteenth chapter is mostly devoted to an account of Amaziah, the contemporary king of Judah, who foolishly challenged Jehoash to engage in a war which ended in the fall of Jerusalem to the forces of Israel, when much damage was done to its walls, and the temple was looted. The chapter ends with a very brief account of Jeroboam II, the third and greatest king of the dynasty of Jehu.

Israel after Jehu — Two Kings Turn to Prayer

The two chapters under discussion here are dominated by an account of the dynasty of Jehu which, we have already noted, lasted longer than any other in Israel's history. The writer suggests to us one reason why God allowed it to survive so long. Neither of the two kings who followed Jehu were outstandingly pious. Neither showed any repentance before God for the sins of Jeroboam which continued to blight their national life (cf. 13:2, 11). Yet, by the grace of God one extraordinary feature marked the reigns of both. Each of them had to endure periods of intense suffering under the hand of Hazael when they felt that even the survival of their nation came into question. Each of them in his need, however, resorted to prayer. We read of one especially dramatic occasion when *Jehoahaz entreated the LORD and the LORD heeded him... Therefore the LORD gave Israel a saviour, so that they escaped from the hands of the Arameans'* (13:4–5). This answer, however, was merely a first sign that God 'heeded' and 'saw' (v. 4) and was ready to respond. It is implied in the narrative that as the need continued the custom of turning towards God continued. Jehoash, the successor of Jehoahaz himself in dire straits gave a sign that he too was turning to God for help when he sought out Elisha, even though the old prophet was on his deathbed. He wept and pled for his help and counsel in the continuing battle. God, in answer, we are told again, saved Israel. '*He turned towards them, because of his covenant with Abraham, Isaac and Jacob, and would not destroy them*' (13:23, see note).

Moreover, we are finally told, not only did God begin to answer the prayers of each king during his own lifetime, he also, as a final sign of his favour towards them, enabled their successor, Jeroboam II, at the beginning of his rule to attain a prosperity and political strength unparalleled in the history of the nation (14:26–27, see note).

As we read through to their end the two chapters before us it will be obvious that as he goes through the story he has to tell, the writer is concerned to give his readers a message about the potential effect of prayer in determining the history and welfare of God's people. Here, too, is a testimony to the place it can have in our own lives and the marvellous way it is so often answered. God, he reminds us, pities us in our need, wants to help us, and is easily entreated (13:4). He is, indeed, willing to give us more than we ask, if we will only ask for more (13:18–19). The author, as we will see, affirms that if Israel had only continued to have kings and people who could pray to God like Jehoahaz they would never have suffered the dreadful fate that for generations had threatened them (14:27).

It is illuminating to go through the whole passage, and note the kind of prayer he is describing and the circumstances that inspired such prayer. Prayer to them was not a practised art. Nor did it arise out of strong faith. Their cries to God reflected the haunting desperate uncertainty they felt to be in their situation. After all, Elijah and Elisha had both made it clear that Hazael their oppressor had been raised up by God to scourge them for their past apostasy: *'The anger of the Lord was kindled against Israel; so that he gave them repeatedly into the hand of King Hazael of Aram'* (13:3).

Their praying was simply a matter of asking for God's help with desperate urgency in a situation that gave them no other ground for hope except from God. It was a last resort when everything seemed to be lost. Left to their own human resources, they were facing certain defeat with horrific consequences from a brutal and merciless enemy. Their only hope was that God might have mercy. Jehoahaz in the midst of the battle simply *'entreated the Lord'* hoping to move him finally to pity with his importunate asking and desperate plight (13:4). Jehoash was weeping when he went to the deathbed of Elisha (13:14) not only because he knew he was about to lose an adviser and friend, but chiefly because the difficulties of kingship in the national situation had driven him to tears, and he was simply clutching at the hope that the dying old prophet would guide him as he groped for help in the direction of God.

That this was the kind of praying that it pleased God to answer so generously, brings before us one basically important aspect of the teaching of the Bible about prayer. We have many examples of it: 'They cried to God in the battle, and he granted their entreaty because they trusted in him' (1 Chron. 5:20).

The impression is sometimes given and received that prayer in its best and most acceptable form is an art that can be learned, essentially the cultivation of communion with God, coming to perfection when the soul and will are at rest in him. Prayer is often discussed today as the cultivation of 'spirituality'. It is regarded as an important aspect of our human nature which must be nurtured and developed if we are to live fully human lives. Certainly the Bible stresses the immense importance of cultivating a thankful and personal relationship with God for the enjoyment of which we were made. It emphasises that a beautiful Church liturgy can be a worthy offering in his name. Yet it reminds us continually that in any relationship we have with God, as Luther once said, 'We are always beggars', and the more genuine the fellowship with him becomes the more urgent and even desperate our begging becomes. With God we never get beyond a relationship in which we ourselves have nothing and God always has everything.

'I need thee every hour
    in joy or pain;
Come quickly and abide,
    or life is vain'.

We have to remember that Jesus, 'in the days of his flesh ... offered up prayers and supplications, with loud cries and tears, to the one who was able to save him' (Heb. 5:7). His chief examples of praying were of two distracted and distracting people (cf. Luke 11:5–8, 18:1–5). The one is of a man who desperately needs bread for a hungry friend, knocking persistently on a neighbour's door at midnight, shamelessly disturbing the sleepy occupants till they are aroused. The other is of a woman who has been cruelly wronged, continually and persistently waylaying a judge and crying out to him to help her. Both are examples of the same desperate and urgent asking arising out of our always critical life-situation. Jesus when he referred to prayer nearly always implied that it was basically and simply an asking.

Israel after Jehu — Elisha is Still There!

When Jehu was anointed to take over rule in Israel, Elisha retired gracefully. He must have become well aware that there was now no place for him in the leadership of national affairs. He had been called by God to supplement and complete the mission of Elijah. That phase in the work had now come to an end, and he was wise enough to know that Jehu was unlikely ever to consult him. Moreover, the inspiration to act through miraculous signs that had established this prophetic leadership also seemed to cease. Possibly he was glad to retire, believing that his appointed work was done. He must have continued to express his deep concern for the welfare of Israel, at the mercy of such a man as Hazael, in constant prayer. He lived on for many years. Jehu reigned for twenty-eight years, and Jehoash for seventeen. He died under Jehoahaz.

Though Jehu ignored him, we can well imagine, however, that under the recurring later national emergencies in the reigns of Jehoahaz and Jehoash and the new religious impulses that marked these reigns, he would again be consulted. Jehoahaz, during the emergencies that drove him to prayer, must have found him helpful, and many scholars think that the incident recorded in the eighth chapter of our book (vv. 1–6) where an unnamed king asks the members of his court to tell him the stories of Elisha, actually belonged to this period of his history and has become misplaced in the narrative (see note p. 106). In his old age he found that the honoured name which he himself had once accorded to Elijah, '*the chariots of Israel and its horsemen*', (13:14, cf. 2:12) was now transferred to himself in the minds and talk of his admirers.

This gives us the setting in which we can best understand the visit paid to him when he was on his death-bed, by Jehoash. It was at the height of a national emergency. Many features of the occasion of the king's visit — his expression of anxiety, his reference to the 'chariots and horsemen', his desolating grief at his impending future loss — must have brought back vividly to the mind of the old man, the day when he too had found himself in a situation so similar! He himself had felt just like this youngster on the day when Elijah was to be taken from him! The thought came to his mind: Was there not here a call to him from God to help and inspire this man before him as Elijah had helped him in his sense of dire need on that last walk together beyond the Jordan? Might not God again, here and now, make a dying old man the same source of marvellous wisdom and inspiration as had happened there and then? He must have prayed. God heard him and through one last marvellous sign brought his long career to a fitting climax.

He must have been thrilled by the very prophecy God gave him to deliver. He was given the assurance that God was now going to bring to an end the power of Aram to harass Israel, and was indeed ready to punish them for ripping up their pregnant women and dashing to pieces the little children (see chapter 8:12 and note). He knew also that he had been entrusted with the task of giving this good news to the king and of inspiring him with the zeal to overcome his nervousness and to go courageously into battle. He felt himself inspired to convey the great news to the king in a symbolic action which was itself designed to ensure the very fulfilment of the prophecy (see p. 16). '*Take a bow and arrows*', he said. Then the command came '*Draw the bow*'. As the king obeyed, Elisha '*laid his hands on the king's hands*'. The next command was: '*Open the window eastward*', then '*shoot*'. Then as the arrow sped in the direction of Damascus came the explanation to the young king of the whole act: '*The arrow of victory over Aram, for you shall fight the Arameans in Aphek until you have made an end of them*'.

The symbolism, of course, was all designed to help the young king to grasp the full implications of what God was saying to him at that very moment. That the prophet put his hands so decidedly on his own hands and directed the shot was a promise of God's presence, guidance and inspiration during the forthcoming battles — an assured triumph! Elisha himself was greatly moved by assurance that at last God was going to show such favour to Israel, but he felt that the response of Jehoash to the challenge seemed to lack enthusiasm. The young king had not caught the thrill of the moment and seemed not fully to have grasped the wonder of the presence of God, and the message. His last effort was an attempt to rouse him. '*Take the arrows,*' he ordered, and '*strike the ground with them*'. Disappointingly Jehoash again failed to rise to the occasion, and as if questioning what was happening '*he struck three times and stopped*'. His action was listless and he seemed aimless. We are told that '*the man of God was angry*'. Had he struck six times Aram would have been duly destroyed. As it was he had given himself a limited scope for victory by his lack of zeal.

Perhaps Elisha remembered a like moment at the beginning of his career when the impulse had come to him to strike the waters of Jordan so that God could demonstrate there and then his presence and his power. He remembered how he had been inspired to accept the challenge of his situation and had struck the water with all his strength and called on the Lord God of Elijah and the waters had parted before him. His deep disappointment with Jehoash was that with his listless and almost bewildered response he had failed to allow himself to be caught up into the spontaneous enthusiasm God was seeking from him at that unique and significant moment of his life.

We can interpret Elisha's anger as directed not simply and personally against Jehoash but against all those of us who allow ourselves to be held back from the full achievement of what God is seeking to do for us and through us by the same listless spirit and lack of sensitivity. We are reminded in this whole incident of how much God can do for us and give us in a moment. As we have already seen from our study of Joash, the faithful observance of routine business becomes an important aspect of the service of God. Yet in the midst of the routine there can arise moments in which God comes near especially to press his claims upon us and to assure us. He wants to give our lives fresh direction and to rekindle our zeal. As well as being faithful in the duties of our calling it is important that we must be always sensitive to and open to such a challenge.

Israel after Jehu — the Door of Hope is Closed

Towards the end of the two chapters before us the writer introduces us to the conditions prevailing in Israel at the beginning of the reign of Jeroboam II. He writes as if God indeed is answering the prayers of his two pious predecessors who had given him and his kingdom a glorious opportunity to retrieve the past failure and shame that had blighted his nation's past, and to make a fresh start. Yet he tragically has to report that Jeroboam did evil. He returned wholeheartedly to *'all the sins of Jeroboam son of Nebat which he caused Israel to sin'* (14:24). He did not spend time at this point giving us the details of this long and evil reign. His readers would be familiar with the grim details given in the written prophecies of Amos and Hosea which were current still in their time. Mammon had in turn replaced Baal as the god of Israel and its worship had given rise to devastating self-centredness, faithlessness and social cruelty.

With all this in mind, as he gives us his closing thoughts about the dynasty of Jehu, he dwells in two especially significant verses (see 14:26 and 27) on the intensity and absurdity of the tragedy that took place under Jeroboam II. The blessing poured out on Israel in answer to desperate prayers had been intended by God to open up before it a new and glorious era in God's service. God, he insists, had always been ready to be good to Israel. He had never intended its past history of shame. He *'had not said that he would blot out the name of Israel from under heaven'* (14:27). His grace and goodness under Jehoahaz and Joash show that at the start of the reign of Jeroboam II Israel had been brought to the verge of a glorious new future. God had remembered his covenant with Abraham, Isaac and Jacob that they should bring blessing to all mankind (13:23) and had been seeking again to take them back to himself so that these promises could be fulfilled. But, instead, in spite of the now open door and the goodness of God, they had deliberately again chosen the way of self-destruction.

He is reminding us, his readers, that our God, the God of Israel, always was and is 'the God of hope' (Rom. 15:13), never the God of fate or of any changeless decree. There are no ready-made plans of his that cannot be changed. He has left our future open to be determined by our prayers and decision as we turn to him in repentance and faith. This kingdom of Israel was destroyed because it slammed shut the door of hope in face of a merciful and patiently loving God.

Amaziah of Judah

The writer of the Book of Kings is referring mainly to the beginning of the career of Amaziah when he tells us that *'he did what was right in the sight of the Lord'* (14:3). When he was in the position of being able to take revenge on his father's murderers, he showed great enlightenment and forbearance. It was the traditionally accepted custom that the children of such criminals should be put to death along with their parents (cf. Joshua 7:24ff, 2 Kings 9:26). Here was a king who seemed to be more sensitive to the nature of true justice (see note).

He can be commended, too, for his re-armament programme described so fully in Chronicles (2 Chron. 25:5–6). At the end of his father's reign Judah had been almost defenceless under foreign attack. His expedition against Edom was an economic necessity. Its aim was to secure access to the port at Elath and to restore its continually threatened trade-routes. It was sanctioned by a prophet of the Lord, and we are told that as a condition of this sanction Amaziah agreed to send home a large contingent of mercenaries whom he had hired from Israel. He obediently went to Edom trusting only in God for the extra help he felt he needed (2 Chron. 25:7–10).

The suggestion in the Book of Kings is that when he was flushed up with his success in Edom things began to go wrong. He was emboldened foolishly to declare war on Jehoash of Israel who by this time had recovered from his conflict with Aram and had a tried and stronger army than his own. We find Jehoash wisely reminding him of the well known parable of the thornbush of Lebanon which challenged a great cedar, only to find itself soon trampled down by a passing animal. *'Be content with your glory, and stay at home'* (14:10) was the advice. Amaziah may have interpreted this as a taunt. We know also, from the Chronicles' account, that he was deeply resentful over the behaviour of the Israelite mercenaries whom he had dismissed before he went to Edom. Angry at being made so suddenly redundant, they had plundered some of his villages on their way home (2 Chron. 25:10).

In spite of Jehoash's warning, therefore, Amaziah went into battle. Judah was defeated and Jerusalem was invaded and plundered. A powerful faction, disillusioned and bitter, conspired against him. We are told that when his son Azariah became sixteen, the age when he could legitimately become king, they crowned him instead of his father. Amaziah fled to Lachish where eventually he was murdered (see note).

As in the case of Joash his father, the book of Chronicles gives us extra information about what happened at the turning point in Amaziah's career. It tells us that he had killed his defeated enemies in Edom by throwing them from the top of Mount Sela so that they were dashed on the rocks, that after this slaughter he' brought the gods of the people of Seir, set them up as his gods, and worshipped them' and refused to listen to the rebuke of the prophet of God who condemned him, as he later did to the warning of Jehoash (2 Chron. 25:11–16). It is mentioned in the Chronicles' account, that even when he did what was right, it was 'not with a true heart' (2 Chron 25:2). The kings of Judah, in spite of their higher ideals, are beginning to prove occasionally as foolish and false as those in Israel have been. Here is a second king of Judah, murdered by his subjects!

Notes

13:22–23 *On the Incident at Elisha's Tomb*
We find ourselves content, on reading this story, with the comment of Skinner that his bones could work miracles; for it was reported that on one occasion a dead body flung hurriedly into the prophet's tomb on the approach of a band of marauders was restored to life. The story is simply such an illustration of what people then believed about him, just as e.g. Acts 5:15 is an illustration of what some people believed about Paul even in his lifetime.

14:2 *On the Length of Amaziah's reign*
The Chronology in Kings, cf. 13:10 and 15:1, seems to allow Amaziah only a space of twelve years less than the twenty-nine mentioned here. The apparent confusion of dates is explained in different ways. Some think that the '29' in verse 14:2 has been wrongly transcribed and should read as '19'. Wiseman thinks that Amaziah survived a long time at Lachish and that he could have survived in joint rule with his son for twenty-four years. Others have varied opinions on how to deal with the difficulty. The student should at least be aware of it.

14:6 *On Amaziah's Early 'Enlightenment'*
When this account of Amaziah in the Book of Kings was being circulated in Babylon, the exiles had been seriously asking why they, the children, should be plunged into such deep suffering because of the sins of their fathers. Ezekiel had given a decisive answer from God sympathising with their complaint and accusing them of short-sighted views of God's ways. God, in meting out justice, does not allow 'the son to die for his father's iniquity' (Ezek. 18:17, see whole of chapter). Here is being

held before them the example of a young king of the line of David who also saw more deeply than they to the heart of God's ways. Could it have happened that the writer of Kings toned down the harshness of the full portrait in order to emphasise this particularly good point?

The Dynasty of Jehu

Points for Further Thought and Discussion

It is possible that both Jehoahaz and Joash in their approach to the Lord in prayer were actually stimulated to pray for God's mercy because of the very fact that they were under his judgment. Can we, too, know ourselves close to God, and encouraged to pray for his mercy because we are aware that we are being disciplined by him? Cf. Micah 7:8–9.

God saw 'that the distress of Israel was very bitter... there was... no one to help' (13:26). Meditate on this verse, and also on the pathetic cry from the hapless man in John 5:7, which brought an immediate reply from Jesus.

Does the fact that Elisha in his old age had so much to offer his people in fellowship, encouragement, advice and prayer — an offer that was not fully accepted! — have something to say to us today about our neglect of this potential source of guidance and inspiration within the Church?

The promising beginning and disappointing ending of Jehoash's visit to Elisha shows it possible for a man to weep and pray earnestly out of felt need, and yet lack an entirely wholehearted persistence to take the enthusiastic action God wills in response to the prayer. Do we find ourselves also to blame here? Is there something we must do about it in some area of life?

Think of Amaziah challenging Jehoash to war — foolish, resentful, boastful, having just found a strange self-centred pleasure in the killing field. Read the warning in James (4:1 R.S.V.) that such passions cause fightings among us and can even lead today to wars. Think of our own need for continual self discipline, for prayer, for wise and moderate leadership in international affairs, etc.

Chapter XIII

THE EXILE OF ISRAEL AND THE DECLINE OF JUDAH

2 Kings 15:1–17:41

The Narrative

At the end of chapter 14 and at the beginning of chapter 15, there is mention of Jeroboam II of Israel, and Azariah of Judah. Under both kings who had long reigns both Israel and Judah enjoyed great prosperity. The three chapters which now open before us, however, contain the story of how the fall of Israel, and its disappearance as a political entity, came about (15:8–31; 17:1–6). They also contain reflections on why this happened (17:7–18) and on how the land of Israel became occupied by those who came to be called 'Samaritans' (17:19–41). They contain also an equally depressing picture of what was meanwhile happening in Judah in the reign of Ahaz who eventually succeeded Azariah (16:1–19).

Israel Rejects its Destiny

What happened towards the end of the dynasty of Jehu, during the reign of Jeroboam II, sealed the fate of Israel as a nation. Up till then God had held on to them and had left open a door to a future as his people. The prosperity given to them even at the beginning of this finally decisive reign was a sign of his continuing goodwill for, as we have just read, God did not will 'to blot out the name of Israel under heaven' (14:27). But now it happened. Absurdly and decisively at this very time Israel finally within the brief period of forty years, rejected its destiny and God let it go.

The historian who writes our present account of this tragic happening emphasises, as we shall see, that the fall was due to their enduring unwillingness to forsake the sin of Jeroboam I, the worship of the golden calves at Bethel and Dan, and we will examine his penetrating analysis of the situation later (cf. pp. 154–155). The writings of the three great prophets who lived through the time, Hosea and Amos in Israel and Isaiah in Judah, enable us to supplement what he says, and to discover more immediately apparent aspects of what led to the downfall that took place. World conditions were drastically changing. The Assyrian empire was beginning to extend its dominating influence in their direction, and had destroyed the power of Aram. Freed from their traditional enemy, both Judah, under Azariah, and Israel, under Jeroboam II, became prosperous. The latter 'restored the borders of Israel from Lebo-hamath as far as the Sea of the Arabah' (14:25). Its newly acquired possessions and access to trade routes, as one historian says, brought them, 'a kind of golden age'. The people of Israel were therefore being called graciously and persistently to return to God, to destroy their golden calves, and to seek to live out in their social and religious life the witness to his righteousness and love that it had been their destiny to declare to the world. Here under the blessing of God was a new opportunity to become a blessing to all nations (Gen. 12:1–3).

Instead, God's goodness led to forgetfulness of God (Hosea 13:6) and to more self-destructive idol worship (Hosea 4:12, 8:4). They developed an overweening pride in their successful colonial enterprise (Amos 6:13). The enjoyment of wealth made those who had it, covet more. Competitiveness and harshness began to replace the ideals of sharing and mutual supportiveness that had been meant to mark their social life under God's law. In the midst of a rising living-standard, the rich, instead of being open-handed to the poor, offered them loans, extracted usury and enslaved them when they could not pay. Traders, already wealthy, found means of making excess profits by creating monopolies, and cheating with debased goods and false weights. 'We will make the ephah small', they said to themselves, 'and the shekel great, and practise deceit with small balances, buying the poor for silver, and the needy for a pair of sandals, and selling the sweepings of wheat' (cf.

Amos 8:4–6). Thus the wealth flowed to those who had it, and 'the gold that made one rich, made another poor'.

The feeling that everything was going their way (the 'feel-good factor!') brought an overweening self-confidence. Even when they were visited by a devastating earthquake which should have brought them to repentance, they responded instead with pride: 'The bricks have fallen, but we will build with dressed stones; the sycamores have been cut down but we will put cedars in their place' (Isa. 9:10). The more religiously minded among them took their prosperity as a sign that God, at this stage in their history, had become so pleased with them that they were now on the verge of inheriting his promises of an even more golden age — the day of the Lord! Amos tried to crush their hopes. 'The day of the LORD', he said, would be 'darkness, not light, and gloom with no brightness in it' (Amos 5:20). When it finally came it would bring irretrievable disaster. 'The end has come upon my people Israel' (Amos 8:2).

> 'Fallen, no more to rise
> is maiden Israel,
> forsaken in her land,
> with no one to raise her up'.
>
> (Amos 5:2)

The Decline of the Kingdom and the Fall of Samaria

The decline and fall which followed the death of Jeroboam II, was dramatic and swift. Divisive factions flourished and the downward movement began. During the course of the history, as one commentator remarks: 'Only one of Israel's kings died a natural death and left the succession to his son, who in turn could retain the sceptre only for a short time. Of the others, each one killed his predecessor to gain the crown.'

Zechariah, Jeroboam's son lasted only six months and was assassinated in public by Shallum. After a reign by him of one month, Menahem, another contender for the throne came to Samaria, killed him, and took his place. In quelling the opposition against him Menahem resorted to a practice hitherto unknown in Israel of ripping open all the pregnant women in one city. No wonder he found himself faced by determined opposition within his realm. He had to buy the assistance of the Assyrian emperor to keep him in power and he had to tax his subjects heavily to pay the cost. All his days there was in the land an opposition party led by Pekah — ardently anti-Assyrian. When Menahem died Pekah was able to murder his son and assume sole rule. At this time Judah came under the rule of an indecisive and weak Ahaz, and Pekah, despising all the close and sacred bonds with which God had bound his people to those of Judah entered a conspiracy with the king of Aram to besiege Jerusalem, overthrow the dynasty of David and enthrone there a usurper like himself.

His policy proved disastrous. Tiglath-pileser, the Assyrian king, came and sacked many of his cities and carried the people into exile (15:29). Pekah was murdered by the last king of Israel, Hoshea, who was nominated for the throne by the invading monarch. A remark by the writer suggests that he was in character better than his predecessors (cf. 17:2). His reign lasted nearly ten years, but tragically, attempting to gain some independence by turning towards Egypt for help, he incurred the anger of his patron Shalmanezer, then the new Assyrian king, who took Samaria after a three years' siege and carried all the population away into exile. Isaiah's comments about the pride, drunkenness and gluttony of the population of Samaria at the time of its fall (Isa. 28:1–4) help us to realise that Hoshea had little to encourage him in his continued efforts to resist the final collapse.

The Judas of Judah

When the introduction to Ahaz says that '*he walked in the way of the kings of Israel*', our attention is drawn to the similarity between him and Jeroboam I of Israel. Jacques Ellul points out that the crowning sin of Jeroboam I when he established in the North his own kingdom of Israel was to subordinate his own and his people's religion to politics. As a substitute for the temple at Jerusalem, he built two new sanctuaries within his own borders, one at Bethel, the other at Dan. As a substitute for the Ark he set up in each place a new image for God in the form of a golden calf. 'Here are your gods, O Israel,' he said 'who brought you up out of the land of Egypt' (1 Kings 12:28). He did this because he felt that if his people continued to go up to worship the Lord at Jerusalem, now in enemy territory, they might begin to transfer their loyalty in other matters back to the Davidic regime and his hold over them would be weakened. It involved a complete change in their whole practice of worship, utterly displeasing to God. What was politically expedient had to have priority over all religious considerations.

With Ahaz too, his first concern was to achieve political security in the swiftly changing world around him. When he found his country in danger of attack by a coalition of the armies of Israel and Aram, one prayer alone came to his mind: '*I am your servant and your son*', he wrote to Tiglath-pileser, the king of Assyria, '*come, and rescue me*'. With his petition he sent an offering of silver and gold from both the temple and his own treasury (16:7–8). The priorities which dominated his political and religious policy are clearly revealed in a conversation which he had with Isaiah during the political crisis we have just mentioned. Isaiah pled with him not to turn to Assyria. God himself, he was assured, would support him, and he would soon discover that the threats of his local enemies were empty! To reinforce his promise Isaiah, in the name of God, offered to give him any kind of miraculous proof which might help to dispel any doubt about his word. He pressed him to make a decision on the matter, 'Ask a sign of the Lord your God'. Ahaz's reply was patently self-revealing: 'I will not ask,' he said (Isa. 7:10–12). He was not willing to face any challenge to his settled views or to allow himself to come under any continuing pressure to accept the kind of religion he had decided to reject. He did not want to begin depending on anything in life other than on his skill in political manoeuvre.

Yet religion, kept in its proper place, did interest him. Skinner says that he seems to have been a 'virtuoso in ritual'. After Assyria subjugated Aram, he was summoned to Damascus with other vassal kings to pay tribute to the great Tiglath-pileser.

He was greatly attracted by a type of altar which he noticed there. While staying on in Damascus he sent the exact details of it to Uriah the priest to make a copy of it in Jerusalem where on his return he gave it a prominent place in the sanctuary. He not only presided at its dedication with great solemnity and many sacrifices, but he altered the regular routine of the temple worship to maintain its prominence there. He seems to have instituted special royal offerings. His alterations show a tendency to assimilate the ritual of the temple to that of other nations and religions. At the close of the account of his alterations there is, however, the significant remark: '*He did this because of the king of Assyria*' (16:18). Outside the temple he indulged freely in the '*abominable practices*' of other nations. '*He even made his son pass through fire*' (16:3, see note). It is significant that as life degenerated in Israel they too had begun such practices (cf. 17:7). One commentator reviewing Ahaz' career expresses the view that under him 'Judah sank lower than Israel'. Another points out that history records of him nothing worthy of real respect. He certainly was one of history's successful rogues. It has to be admitted that he managed by sheer compromise to steer his country through a long period of great turbulence without national disaster. But the evil that he did lived after him. During his reign we can trace the beginning of the worst features of the degeneration that showed itself freely and fully during the reign of Manasseh, and finally sealed for Judah the same fate as had happened to Israel.

'They followed the nations that were around them!'

We have described some of the features of the social decline in Israel that made its fall inevitable in the minds of Hosea and Amos. Now in this section of this book before us the writer of Kings gives his own mind on the subject. He is convinced that the corrupting power of false worship was the main factor in their rejection by God.

He goes through the list of the practices to which throughout centuries they had obstinately adhered — the pillars and sacred poles '*on every high hill and under every green tree*' (17:10), the false idols by the worship of which they made themselves false (17:12, 15), the worship of '*all the host of heaven*' (17:16), the passing of their sons through fire, and the use of divination and augury (17:17). Repeatedly of course he mentions the great sin of Jeroboam I in making the images of two calves (17:17, 21–23). Ominously, moreover, he hints at the possibility that Judah, having begun on the same path will eventually follow on to the same fate (cf. 17:19–20). The repetitiveness of his indictment emphasises that their practices had become so habitually embedded in their tradition that in the end there was no hope of their being overtaken by the truth.

Two outstanding sentences in this indictment deserve our special attention. The first is: '*They followed the nations that were around them*' (17:15).

It was only by becoming and remaining different from all other nations that Israel could have been of any use to God. They had been chosen, we remember (cf. Gen. 12:1–2), to be 'blessed' and to share their blessing with the world. This blessing was the quite unique knowledge God gave them, about himself, the meaning of life, and of his purpose for the world. In order to receive this knowledge of the truth, of the way and life which pleased God, they had had to allow themselves to be separated from all other nations, to become different and especially to renounce all the false ideals and idolatries that they had once shared with other peoples. This was why God had kept them so separate when Abraham arrived among the peoples of Canaan, why he had delivered them from Egypt, drawn them apart at Sinai and taught them by themselves in the wilderness for so many years. They had to be made different if they were to fulfil his mission for them. They had to hold on always to the new knowledge and ways that had made them unique. But they had finally refused to be different! This was the reason why God was now casting them off: they had insisted on being 'natural' in their religion — on having exactly the same kind of worship, the same ways of life as other nations had.

The other significant point in the indictment is that when God, as he did continually, sent his prophets to recall them to his truth and his purposes, they '*would not listen*' (17:14).

It had been by his word that he had called Abraham apart, guided his journeying, warned, protected him, promised him future blessings and fulfilled many of his promises. It was by the word that had come to Moses, the voice of God from Sinai and in the tabernacle, that Israel had known his presence in the wilderness and had continually learned his ways. God by his word had continually tried to make them all 'a kingdom of priests, and a holy nation' (Ex. 19:6 R.S.V.). Throughout their history he had sent prophet after prophet to remind them of the word by which they had been called out of darkness to be his chosen race (1 Pet. 2:9). But now they had made themselves deaf to his speaking. It was with persistent and deliberate determination that they made their decision not to listen and to take their own way. The indictment against Israel accuses them of being *'stubborn'* (17:14), in their resistance to God. It implies that they were enthusiastic in their perversity and resentful towards him for attempting to make them so different from other nations. They left God with no alternative than to allow them to take their chosen path to self-destruction for no other reason than that '*they would not take the way he set before them*' (17:14). The cause was in their will (Matt. 23:37, John 5:40).

The analysis given in this chapter of what led the people of Israel to their complete rejection by God reminds us of a warning Jesus once gave his own disciples. It occurred as he was preaching to them his Sermon on the Mount. In it he described the distinctive features that were bound to characterise the way of life and thought of his disciples, and make them quite different from the world around them. To underline how important this difference was, he said to them, 'You are the salt of the earth'. He was referring to the quite distinctive taste that salt has. It was to be their chief concern to uphold and maintain in their way of life and thought everything he was talking about so that the world would clearly recognise, or 'taste', the unique difference between them and itself. But 'if the salt has lost its taste', Jesus added, 'it is no longer good for anything, but it is thrown out and trampled under foot of men!' Woe to them if they ever even thought of trying to be like the 'Gentiles' or the nations round about them. Might Jesus not have been thinking of the fall of Israel and of this chapter, when he uttered such a warning — Israel worthless and trodden underfoot.

We have to be aware of the pressure on ourselves today, and the temptation it carries with it, to become 'like the nations'. It was there even in the early Church, and it had to be resisted. When Paul wrote to the Romans, 'do not be conformed to this world' (Rom. 12:2), he was not calling on Christians of his day to avoid merely the obviously degrading moral behaviour prevalent around them, he was rather referring to what was regarded as best in the religious culture and thought world of their day. Of course there were many things that were good and lovely and just in that ancient world. These were to be pursued (Phil. 4:8). But when it came to matters such as the meaning and purpose of life, and the nature of God, how he is to be found, approached and worshipped, the world was heathen, and there could be no fellowship with it. 'In the wisdom of God', wrote Paul to the Church in Corinth, 'the world did not know God through wisdom' (1 Cor. 1:21). What even its best thinkers and religious men taught about God and truth could not be allowed to stand in the devotion and mind of the Church alongside 'Christ and him crucified' (1 Cor. 2:2) or to become in any way decisive in matters of thought, worship and behaviour.

We ourselves, living under Christ and the New Covenant are put in a position of having to think out what it means to be 'crucified to the world' and to have the world 'crucified to us' (cf. Gal.6:14). When the German Church in the 1930's was showing signs of allowing the influence of the then current Nazi philosophy to change their church life and attitude, a minority among them found they had to resist, and over against this current trend they stated their conviction that 'Jesus Christ is the one word of God', and their refusal to recognise 'other events, powers and images alongside him as divine revelation'. In understanding our mission and shaping our thought, we too have to resist the temptation to *'follow the nations...around us'*.

An 'Establishment' Compromise

The king of Assyria replaced the exiled population by people who had been enslaved and transported from other conquered regions. One of the problems with which they found themselves immediately faced was the danger of attack by lions, the population of which had enormously increased during the years of rural neglect. Public opinion being ignorant of the true origin of the former Israel's religion assumed that the God of Israel was the local god of the land, and, that he must have become angry by being neglected. Therefore the cure they asked from the king of Assyria was that they send a priest from the former population to teach them what kind of god he was and how he was to be worshipped. A former priest from Samaria came and lived in Bethel to teach them.

The result was that '*these nations worshipped the Lord, but also served their carved images*', (17:41). They themselves felt that the amalgamation they had made of their paganism and the religion of Israel was so satisfying and acceptable to God that when the Jews came back from their exile they approached them hoping to join in the re-building of the temple as if they were indeed members of the true people of God. 'Let us build with you', they claimed, 'for we worship your God as you do' (Ezra 4:2). They were angry when their co-operation was rejected, as was inevitable, and their anger soon turned into deadly enmity.

The writer, however, as he reviews the situation is writing with deep sarcasm that such a compromise could even be tried. Here is a people so fuddled in their religious thought, and so compromised in their ways of life that they can imagine such a nationalised and territorialised form of the true faith to be even possible! Perhaps his little touch of humour should be a warning to us today about the dangers that are always there when there is a settled religious establishment.

Notes

16:3–*Ahaz's Child Sacrifice*
The implication is that this was an aspect of indulgence in the worship of Molech involving the actual burning of children in sacrifice (cf. Lev. 18:21). In this practice he imitates the contemporary Kings of Israel (17:17) and he was followed in Judah by Manasseh (cf 21:6, 23:10). Like practices were rare

and condemned during the early history of Israel. They began to threaten life in Israel and Judah only during this period of national apostasy (cf. Mic. 6:7) and come under condemnation by Jeremiah (cf. 7:30–31) and Ezekiel (cf. 16:20–21).

The 'Samaritans' in the New Testament
There is division of opinion on whether there is any relation between these syncretistic worshippers described here and the Samaritan community referred to in the New Testament and visited by Jesus at Sychar on his journey through Samaria. Some, following Josephus, hold that it was the descendants of these settlers who later settled near Shechem, claimed their descent from the patriarchs, and built the rival temple at Gerizim. Other scholars argue that the community mentioned in the New Testament had their origin later, e.g. in a community of separatists desiring to settle where they could cultivate greater purity of religion apart from Jerusalem.

Points for further Thought and Discussion

Safety and prosperity were given by God to Israel so that in gratitude they could turn towards God and witness more clearly to him in a rapidly expanding world. They trusted in their wealth rather than in the giver, and it corrupted their purposes and way of living. Jesus warned us of how difficult it is for a rich man to enter the Kingdom of heaven (Mat. 19:24). Are we ourselves endangered? What does this history suggest as a cure?

The prophets always laid emphasis on what was quite unique and incomparable in the nature, work and will of the God of Israel (cf e.g. Isa. 46:5, Deut. 4:33–39). Today there is a tendency to find what is common to Christianity and other religions in such matters, to make as many points of contact as possible in order to find common ground for fellowship. Do you think this can be a faithful and fruitful approach?

Ahaz, discontented with the traditional imagery and worship in the temple, sought rather to order the form of worship, with ceremonies of his own choice, and to stimulate his religious devotion by products of his own imagination. What matters in worship is that God should accept it, give his presence within it and bless it. He rejected Ahaz decisively. Are we ourselves today courting the same danger when we seek to re-image God, and stimulate feeling and thought by devising new forms of worship?

Cf, 17:15: – *'They went after false idols and became false'*. Is this true of what is happening around us, and perhaps within us in our world today? Contrast 2 Cor. 3:18.

Though we no longer sacrifice our children to Molech, is there much difference between this and e.g. our failure to surround them with healthy discipline, to protect them carefully from drugs, pornography and abuse? Think over the relevance for today of the prayer uttered to Jesus by the royal official in John. 4:49.

Chapter XIV

HEZEKIAH — AN INTIMATE PORTRAIT (1)
2 Kings 18:1–19:37

The Narrative

Hezekiah's reign is described as beginning with great promise. He abolished pagan religious customs, purified the temple and its worship. Moreover, even at a time when the Assyrians were enslaving the Northern Kingdom, he was bold enough to head a local resistance movement against them.

In the fourteenth year of his reign, however, under acute threat, he suddenly reversed his policy, impoverished his treasury and even stripped the temple of its gold to appease the King of Assyria. When the appeasement failed to buy off an attack on his land he found he had again to offer resistance. The narrative contains many details of a dramatic call for the surrender of Jerusalem by an embassy of the Assyrians, it tells of the reaction of the city's delegates, the humiliation and distress of Hezekiah, the word from Isaiah, in the name of God, promising deliverance. Finally we read of a further threatening letter from the Assyrian king, of Hezekiah's confident response of Isaiah's taunt-song, and we are given a vivid description of the city's extensive miraculous deliverance.

Strength in Weakness!

We are now to be introduced to the best and most dedicated of all the descendants of David. It is a striking feature of the

Book of Kings that he should appear only after it has become obvious that there can be no future for God's people under such an institution as the monarchy. The inevitable trend of the whole history of both kingdoms is now that a Manasseh will follow an Ahaz and justify God's decision to end this tragic phase in Israel's history. The people of Judah are already doomed to future exile. They will have intense and prolonged suffering but they will come through it victoriously. They will be taught about God and themselves, about how to endure and understand what has happened to them. They will have prophets to teach them. They will have their age-long tradition of law and folklore to inspire them.

Moreover, when they begin to ask the most difficult questions they will also be able to learn from their immediate past.

The Book of Kings, was written not simply to justify the exile, and to warn against idolatry and falsehood, but also to bring encouragement to the exiles. The writer of Kings has here, we believe, selected from the life of Hezekiah aspects which he knows will be helpful to his perplexed readership as they face the beginning of their time in Babylon.

It is noticeable that the account of Hezekiah in the Book of Kings differs considerably from that in Chronicles. The latter book concentrates on his inspiring natural leadership and on his social and religious achievement. The temple was cleansed and renewed. The people were reminded again that their God was great and good. During the critical days of the Assyrian invasion the king is pictured as nobly leading a successful resistance with courage. The chronicler certainly refers with regret to one or two episodes in his life when his heart became proud, nevertheless, throughout all Judah, Hezekiah 'did what was good and right' (2 Chron. 31:20, see chapters 31–32).

The writer of Kings certainly pays a brief tribute to the courage, independence and initiative shown by Hezekiah during the first fourteen years of his life, reversing the pro-Assyrian policy of Ahaz, cleansing the temple, and becoming, among the surrounding groups of nations, the leader of an anti-Assyrian alliance and bold enough to attack Gaza when it was under Assyrian protection.'*The Lord was with him*', we are told, '*wherever he went*' (18:7–8).

After all this, however, we are given simply an intimate personal portrait of Hezekiah himself, as a man with very ordinary weaknesses, continually struggling with himself, often failing and sometimes beaten, who wins through because under the discipline to which God has subjected him in life he has learned to put his trust in the Word of God alone. The writer concentrates especially on two profound experiences that came to Hezekiah, the one arising out of his political involvement, the other being more purely personal. Both helped him to understand himself more deeply, and to orient his whole heart and mind more fully than ever before in prayer to God.

That both experiences came to him comparatively late in life does not mean that in his earlier days, his faith was not genuine, or that his service was in any way unacceptable to God. The writer seems to be indicating here that there can come to us as individuals, under the providence of God, at any time of life, and even as we face death, experiences of renewal, of deepening commitment and fuller surrender, giving us greater assurance and stronger conviction as life advances.

The happenings that brought about such a change taught Hezekiah a lesson he had never before learned from life. Through them he discovered how foolish and unreliable a person he was, even at his best. Up till then his besetting temptation had been trying to serve God with too much self-confidence. He had been proud of the loyalty he was giving and of the gifts he could put at God's disposal. It was through these harsh and self-revealing experiences that he found he could become truly strong and useful to God only when he ceased to put any trust whatever in his own wisdom, strength or goodness, and began to find everything he needed being given to him by the grace of God alone. Of course as they read or hear of these incidents in the life of this outstanding son of David the exiles knew some of the Psalms and the stories of their patriarchs and of David himself which taught them the same kind of lesson. But here in this recent book about their Kings they saw how the power and grace of the living God was still at work in the same way, in a context very near their own in the stream of life that was still moving them on to their promised future. We too, of course under the same grace in the New Covenant find the same message coming home to us in Paul's self confession, when he discovered, in much the same way as Hezekiah, what qualified him for the service of God: 'I will boast all the more gladly of my weaknesses, so that the power of Christ may dwell in me' (2 Cor. 12:9). God never grows weary of teaching us eternal truths in new and fresh situations.

The Road to Self-discovery

We need not under-estimate the comparative worth of Hezekiah's attainments during the first fourteen years on the time of Judah, surrounded by his close local allies. As king, reformer and resistance-leader, he seemed to have the status of a world-statesman, and his leadership seemed to be widely accepted. But his sphere of activity and influence was deceptively sheltered and limited. He had been encouraged to think too highly of himself and what he had achieved. For various reasons the Assyrians had left him too long alone in his corner of the Middle East, and it had been under a false sense of security that his brave words of faith had been uttered, and his bold leadership against Assyria had been offered. The shock was therefore all the greater when he was put to the test, and compelled to face the emptiness of what had given him so much pride, and the faith of his own self-estimate.

It all happened suddenly. The emperor Sennacherib turned his way. He did not even utter threats. As soon as he began to attack the defenceless outlying parts of Hezekiah's kingdom, the king's courage immediately failed. Hezekiah's own subjects and allies must have been shocked not only by the complete U-turn but also by the abject nature of the apology and the offer of reparations: '*I have done wrong; withdraw from me; whatever you impose on me I will bear*' (18:14). The faithful among his people must have become ashamed at the zeal with which he now robbed even the temple of all its treasures, even stripping the gold from its doors, to buy off his tormentor.

We can imagine the shock to his own self-image — to find himself so ardently now taking exactly the course he had despised his father for following! Moreover he knew that in the eyes of his former dependent allies he had now the status of a coward and a traitor. He could never before have imagined himself going this way — but here he was! The effect on his self-esteem of his next move was equally devastating. The King of Assyria was not bought off as he had hoped. Having been paid so much, he came back for more, and Hezekiah realised he had been not only a coward when he gave in to Sennacherib but also a fool. Therefore he decided to begin again to resist him. There was no heroism in his change of policy and it brought him no pride, for he knew in himself when he took it that it was a resistance inspired more by sheer desperation rather than by courage, or faith. His people when they saw him now preparing Jerusalem for siege must have wondered 'what next?' His enemies, of course, recognised how low the community morale must be under such vacillating and unpredictable leadership. So devoid of any moral quality did Hezekiah indeed seem to have become that they were even encouraged to try propaganda before they applied force, believing that it would become a powerful factor in breaking down the will to resist.

The setting for this last minute effort is vividly described, and the cheap arguments used are given in great detail. The Assyrians professed themselves ready for discussion, and sent forward Rabshakeh at the head of their embassy. They are met by '*Eliakim, son of Hilkiah, who was in charge of the palace, and Shebnah the secretary and Joah the son of Asaph, the recorder*' (18:18). We are meant to notice that there were '*people on the wall*' listening, and that the whole consortium would be overheard and reported through the city. We are meant to notice, too, that the Assyrians had '*called for the King*' (18:18) but that Hezekiah had absented himself. The narrative, indeed, suggests that he had hidden himself somewhere beyond earshot and deeply private, where no report could reach him till the delegates themselves went to tell him what had occurred. Was he trying to maintain what little dignity was now left to him by holding himself aloof? Or was he by this time so conscious of his recent failures that he did not want publicity? Unfortunately by his retreat he left the ground more open for the ridicule, which the people now heard poured out by the Assyrians on his policy and past behaviour, and on the faith he had so ardently professed.

When the delegation came and '*told him the words of the Rabshakeh*' (18:37), it must have been with a sense of personal shame that he '*tore his clothes and covered himself with sackcloth and went into the house of the Lord*'! Before the concourse of the whole people of God, where prophets for generations had stood and said, 'Hear the Word of the Lord', the representative of a petty pagan emperor had been allowed to stand and say, '*hear the word of the great king*'! God's name had been publicly mocked, and his anointed defender of the faith, had not been there to answer and uphold!

The Sheep without a Shepherd!

We do not wonder that the delegates who had undergone the ordeal in front of the city wall had already torn their clothes before they came to Hezekiah. The Rabshakeh had raised searching questions that were deeply troubling their minds. In view of their hopeless military situation, was it realistic for them to continue to boost each other's faith simply by repeating to each other the promises of the Lord about their safety and their future (18:22, 30)? After all, might not the emperor's promise be true that if they would simply surrender, instead of the misery of siege and starvation there would be security, abundance and peace? (18:31–32). Might it not be that this new situation was simply a God-given opportunity for their experience to become enlarged, and their faith to progress in line with his purpose that they should become a blessing to all nations (18:25, 33–35)? In face of such pressure, not only the collapse of their king, but also the silence of Isaiah their prophet, must have added to their perplexity. God seemed to have left them at least for that moment like sheep without a shepherd.

It tends to add relevance to this story, that at different times and occasions in the history of the Church, this kind of situation has recurred. Its faith has grown weak and cold. Faced by similar questions and accusations posed in the name of humanity and progress by an alien world, the sheep of the flock, perplexed, have looked up and found their leadership as hesitant and divided as themselves. Moreover, always, as here, the central and most acute temptation of all is: 'All these I will give you, if you will fall down and worship me' (Matt. 4:9). The world around us today with its secular culture and proud humanist agenda seems to offer to the conventional Christian living on the fringe of Church life, so much more than does full commitment to Christ and a strict adherence to his word! It should help us to realise that there is nothing new in either the perplexity or the temptation.

A Cry from the Depths

Hezekiah was describing especially his own feelings when he gave voice to the lament that they were passing through '*a day of distress, of rebuke and of disgrace*' (19:3). '*Children,*' he added, '*have come to birth, and there is no strength to bring them forth*'. The analogy conveys to us the intense nature of the personal tragedy in which he feels himself involved. He had believed that, at this very time of his life, after years of toil, prayer and hope he would be rejoicing to find his kingship fruitful, his people prospering and his faith rewarded by answers to his prayers and tokens of God's blessing, and now he finds himself simply deep in trouble, under reproach from God, and ashamed even to face his own people. We ourselves reading about it, and able to review the whole Biblical story, can realise better than Hezekiah was able to do, how much he was then sharing in common with the great servants of God, who had preceded him. We can think of Elijah, in flight after Carmel (cf. 1 Kings 19:4) sitting down under the broom tree, in the same kind of distress, struggling with the same feelings of rejection at the very moment when he had expected to enjoy the fruits of triumph. We can think of Moses on the mountain (cf. Exod. 32:7,19) at the moment his career was reaching its climax, hearing from God about the golden calf, so shattered by the news of his failure that he smashed the tables of the law against the mountain. We can think of place after place in the Psalms where the writers reveal themselves as passing through such days of '*distress*' (Ps. 88:1–3), '*rebuke*' (Ps. 38:1, 130:1–3) and '*disgrace*' (Ps. 31:10–11).

That he felt himself under 'rebuke' from God was obviously the most acute element in his experience. He went to the temple but he found himself unable even to pray . Had God not hidden his face from such an unreliable and futile man? And had he not lost all claim to his help? He sent a message to Isaiah asking him to pray '*to the LORD your God*' in the hope that the faith of an intercessor might bring him some help. He speaks as if his whole future, and that of Israel too, rests on the flimsy supposition: '*It may be that the LORD your God heard all the words of the Rabshakeh.*' His own faith can rise no higher.

The Word

The answer to Hezekiah's 'cry from the depths' came to him immediately in the Word of God uttered by Isaiah. It began with a simple personal command '*Say to your master, "Thus says the LORD: Do not be afraid ..."*' (19:5). We are not told whether Isaiah's words were spoken in an orally delivered message or were read from a written missive. We cannot doubt, however, that when he heard them, the king himself heard not Isaiah or the messenger, but God himself speaking to him in the very words of the message. It was the voice of the Lord himself saying 'Fear not'.

God's word when it comes like this to us always brings about what it commands and proclaims. Hezekiah's attitude before God and his relation to the world was immediately transformed. His depression was lifted. He began to find freedom from all useless self-reproach, and from his sense of rejection. He knew himself completely forgiven. He was still no doubt in '*disgrace*' before some of his people whose memories were long and bitter, but he was no longer in '*distress*' or '*rebuke*'. Above all he found himself at last able to pray, and, indeed praying. Twice in the account it is mentioned that he knew himself '*before the Lord*' (vv. 14 and 15 when he spread the letter and then prayed in the temple). God was there 'before him' not only speaking, but also inviting conversation.

The King of Assyria was no less powerfully and personally affected by the same Word of God as transformed Hezekiah. '*I myself will put a spirit within him, so that he shall hear a rumour and return to his own land: I will cause him to fall by the sword in his own land*' (19:7). It was several years before everything decreed here was accomplished, but the process began immediately. From the moment Isaiah spoke, the movements of the king of Assyria were like those of a fish on a hook unable to go where it wants, and pulled about here and there against his will (cf. 19:28). Sennacherib wanted there and then to begin the siege of the city, but he was forced temporarily to withdraw his army. Angry at having to retreat he sent a letter to warn Hezekiah that he was about to come back, and redefining now, as he thought indelibly, all the demands his envoys had already made, still hoping for a surrender. It was when the letter reached its destiny that we begin to see the evidence of the transforming effect of the same Word of God in Hezekiah himself, That he '*went up to the house of the LORD' and spread it before the LORD* is a gesture of great significance and eloquence. The whole action is itself a prayer. In making it Hezekiah is spreading before the Lord not only the written parchment but his whole life-situation. He is now inviting God, who has the eyes to see and read, as well as the ears to hear (19:16), to understand these threats and tensions under which he is living and to meet all the need that is here confronting him (cf. Phil. 4:6-7). Sennacherib in dictating his letter has indeed provided Hezekiah with most eloquent means of fellowship with God. Besides asking God to read the letter, all Hezekiah has to do, is now to remind him of all the promises by which he has caused his people through the ages to trust him, '*O LORD our God, save us, I pray you, ... so that all the kingdoms of the earth may know that you O LORD, are God alone*' (19:19).

There is much here that we ourselves are meant to take in, live by, and practise! A mere 'word' did it. It was not heard to sound directly and marvellously from heaven like the voice that was heard when Jesus was baptised or transfigured. It came from God through the mind and mouth of another man. We can think of other occasions when a word that altered the course of history and the life of a soul came in such a way. Hannah went one day to the temple to pour out her agony and prayer for herself and Israel before God. And she heard a word. It was the promise from God of a child. Though it came from an old priest at the altar, its utterance altered human history — for the child to be born was the great prophet Samuel whose ministry renewed and altered the whole course of Israel's history. Moreover, on hearing it, all Hannah's depression and psychological distress was immediately banished. Under the stress of life today we are apt to forget that God means this still to happen. We need not in any way despise the work and art of our modern 'counsellors'. Yet, a word from God, and we can still seek one, can probe to ills that lie in a quite different and deeper dimension of life than those for which our counselling methods are devised, and can still today heal such disorders with miraculous power.

We are meant, as we read on, to appreciate the pastoral care, and indeed the skilful 'counselling' which God actually gave to Hezekiah through the eloquent oracle with which Isaiah answered his prayer. Though the king knew himself forgiven and restored to fellowship with God he was in need of continued encouragement after the long and terrifying ordeal to which Sennacherib had subjected him. Isaiah's inspired oracle is well described by scholars as a 'taunt song'. In it God takes all the boasts which Sennacherib has repeated time and again as he has moved about conquering the world, always with the image of himself dragging his captive peoples into exile with hooks in their noses. The threats are repeated exactly as they were uttered, but they are all mocked. I know your whole story, God is saying, '*Your arrogance has come to my ears*' (19:28) and 'now I am going to put a hook in *your* nose!' What more eloquent way could have been found of saying, 'Fear not', to Hezekiah? The prophet is ridiculing not just Sennacherib but the fears of Hezekiah. The King in his prayer had pled with God to look and listen (19:16) to this tyrant. God now assures him, '*I have heard your prayer*' (19:20), I have seen and heard Sennacherib, too! — and as if the oracle was not enough, the promise that inspired his prayer is repeated, and a sign is given that it will ultimately be fulfilled.

Chapter XV

HEZEKIAH — AN INTIMATE PORTRAIT (II)
2 Kings 20:1–21

The Narrative

Two further important incidents in Hezekiah's life are here recorded. A sudden sickness brings him to death's door and he makes a marvellous recovery. He is visited by ambassadors sent with good wishes by an aspiring king of Babylon. His trusting and open-hearted acceptance of them as prospective war allies brings a rebuke from Isaiah who prophesies the eventual exile of Israel to Babylon.

Again in the Depths — Sickness, Disillusionment, and the Fear of Death!

Hezekiah, in the ordeal here described, is searched and tested in an entirely different area of life than the political, and on an even more deeply personal level. It all happened when he was struck down by what seemed to be a mortal sickness.

We will therefore find him closer to ourselves than he was when we saw him previously struggling with the problems of his political leadership. We all have sometimes close and dear relatives who find themselves under sudden sentence of death at the prime of their lives, their hopes of a promising career (often in the service of God) suddenly shattered by a fatal medical diagnosis! The king here when this happened had seemed to be at a high point in his career, (see note) and was confident, that the prophet, when he made his visit, would pray, and he would be cured. Instead, he heard himself irrevocably sentenced to death: *'You shall die, you shall not recover'*.

The searching challenge which accompanied the sentence to death, also made Hezekiah abruptly face questions that are as pointed and acute for all of us today as they were then for him. '*Set your house in order*', commanded Isaiah (20:1, see note). 'Here Hezekiah,' says one commentator, 'is led out of the city into the royal palace' to face the simple but fateful question: What kind of man had he really been in the home situation? How did his account stand there? Had he shown true faithfulness, consideration and humanity to those with whom God had bound him up intimately within the bundle of life? He was being reminded that the answer to this question counted as much with God as that about his public image or leadership. How urgent it is for all of us to have to face up to exactly this challenge, put to us possibly in these very words!

We find also that the picture of Hezekiah at the point of death turning '*his face to the wall*' is as relevant to us today as were the shock and challenge brought to him by the words of Isaiah. It is a reminder that each of us is entirely alone as we pass through death to face the judgment seat of God. No other soul is there to help us, if God himself is not for us. Luther often used this simple and ultimate fact of life in his preaching to remind his hearers that each must make his or her decision about salvation, here and now, in utter isolation from all others. No one else can give an answer for us, and we ourselves cannot give an answer for anyone else. 'I cannot stand with you, and you cannot stand with me' was often his message, as he made his appeal to each individual to know and rejoice there and then that Christ had died for each one, and was their advocate.

Confidence before God

God heard the prayer and saw the tears of Hezekiah. He cut short his bitter desolation of soul. Marvellously he was on his feet again within a few days, grateful for the promise of fifteen more years of life. We have a brief account of the prayer he uttered out of the depth of his experience (20:3), and in the book of Isaiah we are given the song of thanksgiving which he wrote after his recovery. In this he describes in greater detail what he endured, and the thoughts that ran through his mind

(Isa. 38:9–20). The study of this song can be of great help to us as we try to interpret the present text.

It is to be noted that in this trial he does not in any way experience the pusillanimous self-reproach and the overwhelming sense of guilt, that marked his previously recorded trial. There is here a deep strain of confidence before God as he seeks in prayer to recover from the shock and disappointment to which he feels he has been subjected. The word upholds him, continually within a living and close relationship with God. He is, indeed, so conscious of having the love of God, and of being under his watchful care (cf. 20:3) that he can pour out before him even the bitterness of his heart (Isa. 38:15, 17). As he goes through a period of questioning and resentment he complains freely and confidently about his feeling of utter helplessness (Isa. 38:13 — he has 'all his bones broken', and is 'brought to an end') and his weariness and perplexity (Isa. 38:14–15) under the trial, knowing that God himself will understand.

We have to note how freely and naturally in this present trial, he speaks of himself as a redeemed individual before God. As we watched him in the previous chapter, the chief concern he expressed was for the salvation of the people of God: 'O LORD our God, save us' (19:19). Here, we find, the 'we' and the 'our' have been replaced by 'I' and 'my': 'The LORD will save me' (Isa. 38:20). Not only is he conscious that God has cast all his sins 'behind his back' (Isa. 38:17), he also expresses the faith that God has the personal supervision and control over all the suffering that is allowed to come to him: 'he himself has done it' and even this was his plan for his salvation (Isa. 38:15, 17). He will live in gratitude for those fifteen extra years of life that have been granted to him and will seek throughout them to glorify and enjoy God, and to be a witness to his goodness to the coming generation (Isa. 38:19).

The Struggle Towards Greater Assurance

If his song and his prayer show us how far he has progressed at this stage of his life, they also show us how far he has to go to reach the level of assurance into which we believe that God was then seeking to draw him. While he is full of gratitude for the measure of life and liberty God was granting him, he is at the same time longing for more than he dares to ask. The reader of his song will have noticed how one ingredient of his bitter suffering make it especially difficult to bear when he finds himself under sentence of death. Even though he clung so passionately to God himself, his mind was tormented by the conviction, currently held by the great majority of his people, that God's wonderful fellowship could be enjoyed only during the short years of this present life on earth. After death, in the realm of Sheol, it was believed, this bliss would end:

'For Sheol cannot thank you
    death cannot praise you;
Those who go down to the Pit
    cannot hope for your faithfulness'
              (Isa. 38:11, 18).

We can understand how this belief tended deeply to modify even his present experience of God's goodness because he knew he would too soon be deprived of it.

Many scholars when they comment on this and other like passages in the Bible explain that the attainment of a better life with God, through the resurrection of the dead to glory, was reached only very late in the history of the people of God. A much used and conservative *Dictionary of the Bible* makes the assertion that 'nowhere does a psalmist attain to an assured belief in resurrection', though the 'germ of what remains simply a hope may be found' in some Psalms. We find ourselves questioning this low estimate. Some of the Psalms and other passages of Holy Scripture which may have an early date, seem to us to point quite positively towards a belief in blessedness after death (cf. *Readings in I Kings* pp. 20–21). We find it unnecessary to regard the twenty-fifth chapter of Isaiah's book as being of very late origin, and we believe that the story of the Ascension of Elijah was current in some places even at the time of Hezekiah. Certainly the prevalent view of life after death was in many places negative and comfortless. But a sometimes unexpressed hope in something much better was an ingredient of the piety of many people even in the age of Hezekiah.

Possessed by it they found themselves in conflict with the prevalent view and occasionally in the struggle their faith rose to glorious heights of expectation, just because it was so assailed.

Hezekiah, we believe, is here involved in this struggle. In this poem he is expressing a view he is beginning to find intolerable because he is on the verge of new hope. While he is expressing it he is questioning it and struggling towards the truth God is seeking to have him enjoy. We therefore regard his self-expression under this experience as a pointer towards New Testament hope rather than as a sign of what is asserted to be Old Testament darkness.

His request for a sign, and Isaiah's response to it, is a further reminder of the struggle that the king had to attain and hold on to the full assurance that God meant his word to give him. We ourselves today are urged to be content with a faith that finds its power and assurance mainly by hearing the Word of God (Rom. 10:17, see questions). When God spoke to people by the prophets, however, he often added signs that were sometimes themselves quite miraculous, in order to encourage them to believe the promises he had spoken. Indeed, realising their need of help towards belief he sometimes challenged them, when they had difficulty, to ask for a sign (cf. Isa. 7:11). Hezekiah at this point in his struggle felt this need for help and asked: '*What shall be the sign that the Lord will heal me?*' (20:8).

Ahaz his father had evidently constructed an upper court in the temple or palace in which the shadow cast by the sun, falling on a graduated flight of steps was used, like a sundial, to give a rough idea of the time of day. We need not imagine that the sun itself advanced and then retreated in the heaven to produce this quite localised miracle. It is enough simply to believe that God took marvellous control of the refraction of light on the steps. The shadow cast by the light was first suddenly advanced and then retarded a space corresponding to ten intervals. Hezekiah's special problem was whether or not God could really postpone the ordained day of his death and thus make time retreat rather than advance, and Isaiah in arranging the order of the miracle drew the king's attention to this aspect of the sign. He announced it as specially designed by the Lord to meet his case (20:9 — a '*sign to you from the Lord*'!) We are meant, no doubt, to note his pastoral concern that the very nature of the miracle should be of help to the king's struggling faith.

A Significant Lapse

It is the Book of Chronicles that gives us helpful information about how Hezekiah responded to God, as he grew wealthy after his recovery from sickness and the siege of Jerusalem: 'He did not respond according to the benefit done to him, for his heart was proud' (2 Chron. 32:25). It adds that there came a time when 'God left him to himself, in order to test him and to know all that was in his heart' (2 Chron. 32:31). These comments help us to interpret what happened when King Merodach-baladan of Babylon sent his envoys to Jerusalem on a diplomatic mission. It must have taken place late in the life of Hezekiah. Such a date alone fits in with what we otherwise know from world history (see note). Babylon was at this time a comparatively small kingdom under Assyrian domination but its king was anxious to court the friendship of other powers which, he thought, could help him to form an anti-Assyrian alliance. When the foreign ambassadors arrived, Hezekiah was obviously flattered and excited at having been taken so seriously as a possible ally by a power he regarded as of some potential in world politics. He desired to impress and become accepted. He opened his treasure house, showed all his wealth and displayed his potential military power.

We can only imagine from his behaviour that by this stage in his life he has forgotten the lesson which God has laboured throughout his life to drive home to him by patient, loving and stern discipline: that the people of God can become truly prosperous and blessed only when they look to God alone for protection and strength, and refuse to place their confidence 'in the flesh' (cf. Jer. 17:5). He has begun to fall from grace.

Isaiah must have realised when he was not invited to meet the delegation that something was wrong, and he arrived at the palace too late. We can imagine what he felt when he heard the explanation. More than any other king since David, Hezekiah had seemed to respond well to God's discipline and love. He had inspired hope that God might yet spare the

Kingdom of Judah the fate that had come to the people of North Israel. It did not require much prophetic insight for the disappointed prophet now to foretell the ultimate doom of Judah too. It would not take too much foresight or astuteness to make the suggestion that God was testing the king with a representative of the very power that was so soon to bring it about.

It sounds both callous and self-centred that Hezekiah should so clearly express his satisfaction that the coming disaster should visit his children and grandchildren rather than himself. Wiseman has suggested that we are to read his remark simply as a submissive acceptance of God's Word rather than as an expression of relief at the postponement of the judgment. We, rather, interpret it simply as a momentary expression of the kind of thought that can spring into the mind of any of us at times when we are off our guard, and forget to be our conventional respectable selves. They often make us ashamed of ourselves for even having them (cf. Psalm 51:5) even though we ourselves tend to crush and disown them. Jesus himself spoke of such words as the 'careless' (NRSV) or 'idle' (AV) words that at times we even utter, and which are a serious indication of what we really are at heart (cf. Matt. 12:36). When we hear Hezekiah, off his guard for a moment, saying this kind of thing, we are meant simply to realise that none of us is any less frail than he was.

Notes

Critical questions
In our treatment above, we have interpreted Chapters 18–19 as containing the account of one continuous campaign of Sennacherib against Judah. This evidently took place in two stages, the one being marked by the propaganda assault by Rabshakeh at the walls, the second by the letter from Sennacherib. This campaign found its climax in one miraculous deliverance of Jerusalem under its final siege. A student will be aware of the theory that these two chapters, rather, are the amalgamation of the accounts of two quite distinct events, the one extending from 18:17 to approximately

19:9, the other extending from 19:9 to 19:35. Which theory is chosen, would make only a slight difference to the exposition we have given.

There are problems also attached to the timing of Hezekiah's sickness and the visit to him of Merodach-baladan from Babylon. Hezekiah died in 698 B.C. If after it he recieved sixteen more years of life, its date must have been around 714 B.C. There were two periods during which Merodach-baladan was in power in Babylon. The more likely was from 721–710 B.C. which might place his visit even before the invasion of Sennacherib to Judah which is dated in Hezekiah's fourteenth year, round about 701. This is, however, the possibility that the visit was made during a short tenure which he had of the throne of Babylon in 703, nearer to the end of Hezekiah's life, as is suggested in the arrangement given here by the author of Kings. We have assumed therefore that the visit was late. It has to be accepted that the comment 'after these things' at the beginning of chapter 20, does not necessarily prove that the sickness of Hezekiah took place after the invasion of Judah by Sennacherib. If the sickness did take place earlier than this then we can interpret the humiliation it brought to Hezekiah as an early foretaste of the greater political trial that he was going to have to face. The Book of Chronicles tells us that it was only after both trials, the personal and the political that Hezekiah 'humbled himself for the pride of his heart' (2 Chron. 32:26).

On 19:29–32. The sign given to attest Isaiah's oracle was a quite natural series of events that would occur as the prophecy itself was fulfilled. The Assyrians had been in the land long enough to destroy one harvest. This would leave to mature only the seed that was already by chance lying on the ground. The Assyrians would stay long enough to prevent the sowing of the next year's crop, but in the third year all will be natural.

On 19:34 *'The City of God'*

Two or three generations later when Jerusalem was under siege again, this time by Nebuchadnezzar, king of Babylon, many in Jerusalem interpreted the words of Isaiah here as an assurance that God would not allow the earthly city Jerusalem ever again to fall to an earthly enemy, and they quoted this prophecy against Jeremiah when he advised them wisely, not to resist the Babylonians. They were wrong. Yet we cannot blame them too severely for taking the assurance they did from Isaiah's words, for his prophecy can superficially be read as if it actually guaranteed the future inviolability of the earthly Jerusalem. We believe that Isaiah however had even at the time he uttered the prophecy, more in mind than the future of the earthly city, Jerusalem.

The Old Testament prophets sometimes were inspired to move in their thoughts from things that were happening around them, or were soon to happen in their present age, to greater and more wonderful things that were eventually to happen in a coming Messianic age when God's Kingdom would finally break into the world and all the promises given to the people of God would be finally fulfilled. They were inspired with the belief that some of the events that were being unfolded before them in their present world-history were actually going to be repeated in a more spectacular and glorious way when the true 'Son of David' would come and rule over his people in glory. God, they believed, would then in these final days do a series of great 'new things' (cf. Isa. 42:9, 43:19) parallel to the old things that had at times already happened in the earthly history of Israel. They thought in this way for example when they were told by God to expect soon the end of their imprisonment in Babylon. The new exodus that they were to experience was already like the former exodus from Egypt, but it was to be followed by a new and more glorious eventual exodus of the people of God from all sin and evil bondage. The New Testament speaks not only of such an exodus having been fulfilled in Jesus, it also speaks of a new entrance in him into an eternal promised land, and of course it speaks of the glory and security of the New Jerusalem, the eternal city of God.

It is our belief that when Isaiah uttered the word of God, *'I will defend this city to save it for my own sake and for the sake of my servant David,'* his mind was already being lifted in vision towards things to come. Luther when he wrote his great hymn about the inviolate 'City of God' and we ourselves when we rejoice in having found ourselves through grace members 'of Zion's city', are correctly interpreting Isaiah's prophecy.

On 19:35–37. There is an account by the historian, Herodotus, of a battle which Sennacherib lost to an Egyptian army. Field mice are said to have gnawed at the thongs of the soldiers' shields and bows, making resistance to their enemy impossible. If Egyptian forces came to the help of Hezekiah during the siege at Jerusalem, this kind of happening may have entered the tradition to which Herodotus was refering. Some other kind of plague may be referred to. The 'angel of the Lord' is on another occasion associated in the Bible with pestilence (2 Sam. 24:15f.).

Wiseman here mentions the suggestion that the 'one hundred and eighty five thousand' can be translated as 'one hundred and eighty five officers' who became 'all dead bodies' The two brothers are said to have slain Sennacherib their father because he had named another brother, Esarhaddon, to succeed him.

On 20:1. Ahithophel when he knew his situation had gone beyond recovery, went home, 'set his house in order' and hanged himself (2 Sam 17:23). In the case of David, preparing for death involved giving a 'last charge' to his successor (1 Kings 2:1f.).

On 20:7. The 'lump of figs' was a standard poultice used for medicinal purposes.

Points for further thought and discussion

We have interpreted Hezekiah as one of the outstanding Old Testament men of God who 'won strength out of weakness' (cf. Heb 11:34) He learned to trust in God only when his own self-confidence was shattered. Christ overcame the world by accepting the humiliation, shame and weakness of the Cross. (cf. the 'distress, disgrace and rebuke' of 19:3!). Can the Church ever be strong in his service when it is in anyway self-confident and anxious to display its human resources and strength? What about ourselves?

Think of the implications (for today) of the fact that the Church in those days was hopelessly beaten by the world in the mass media propaganda battle, but easily won in the prayer battle.

Is our praying for Church and personal affairs as close to life as Hezekiah's was when 'he went up to the house of the LORD and spread it (the letter) before the LORD' (19:14, cf. Phil.4:6).

The New Testament in several places suggests that we, too, put our house in order, in view of the fact that the time before us may be short. Study e.g. 1 Cor 7:29–34. Do we heed this enough?

We have to depend on God's word rather than on signs, and in the New Testament we are warned against becoming too anxious about them or too dependent on them. (cf. Mat. 12:38–39). Yet God gave the trembling faith of Hezekiah, in his weakness, a sign when he asked one. Could he possibly be less gracious to us if occasionally we are in the same kind of need today? What should we expect?

CHAPTER XVI

JOSIAH
2 Kings 21:1–23:30

The Narrative

One whole chapter is devoted to a description of the corrupting influence of Manasseh and Amon his son on the religious practices and moral life of Judah over a period of nearly sixty years, confirming the decision of God to give his people up to their enemies. Under these circumstances Josiah at eight years old begins his reign. From the beginning he did what is right and went to work repairing the temple. The decisive period of his reign begins when a 'book of the covenant' which was found by the high priest in the temple was brought to his palace and read to him. He found himself gripped by fear under its condemnation of all the religious abuses that were being tolerated within his realm, and its threats of impending punishment. In repentance after consultation with Huldah, a prophetess, he felt impelled to convene an assembly of all the important people in the land, and had the book publicly read to them. He found he had enough public support to begin a radical reformation in the worship of God not only through his whole realm but also in the territory of the former Northern kingdom. The reforms were carried out with a ruthlessness that inevitably created much redundancy and resentment, and sometimes involved human slaughter. They were remarkably effective. Josiah felt it was his duty to block the passage through the Holy Land of the Egyptian army under Pharaoh Necho. He risked his life and his army, and perished, allowing the Egyptian king such a control of his kingdom's affairs that his religious policy was reversed, and people returned to their old ways.

Judah under Doom, God under Stress!

Even though Hezekiah had tried throughout his life to be a good king, and God had given during his reign a marvellous sign of his love for Jerusalem, his Holy City, yet from the very beginning of his rule his kingdom was on the way to ruin. Ahaz his father had already introduced into Judah all the corrupting beliefs and practices that had sealed the doom of Israel, and these had already taken firm and fatal root in the minds and hearts of the common people in both town and country (cf. 17:13–14, 19).

Even in those days, Isaiah describes as incurable the social and political corruption arising out of such idolatrous paganism:

'The whole head is sick,
    and the whole heart faint.
From the sole of the foot even to the head,
    there is no soundness in it,
but bruises and sores
    and bleeding wounds' (Isa. 1:5–6).

Micah his contemporary who also lived in Judah, and foresaw the fall of the Holy City (cf. Mic. 3:12), could write from his observation of society around him:

'Their hands are skilled to do evil;
The official and the judge ask for a bribe,
and the powerful dictate what they desire,
    thus they pervert justice ....
Put no trust in a friend,
    have no confidence in a loved one;
Guard the doors of your mouth
from her who lies in your embrace;
for the son treats the father with contempt.'
               (Mic. 7:3, 5–6).

Any faint remaining hope of better things to come was finally crushed when Manasseh came to the throne. Everything alien to Israel's traditional faith seemed to appeal to him. During his fifty-five years' reign he encouraged the pursuit of all the pagan cults and superstitions of the surrounding world, and allowed the intrusion of heathen altars into every corner of the temple itself (21:3–8). Though before his reign there was a deep inclination towards what was condemned by God (cf. Jer. 5:31), under his leadership he '*seduced*' (cf. 21:9 R.S.V.) the people more firmly till his paganism attained an irreversible hold over their affections.

Moreover, he sought to stifle all opposition by terror. He '*shed very much innocent blood*' (v. 16) in his crusade. The Lord's prophets were slain. There is a legend that it was Manasseh who had Isaiah martyred by being sawn in two. Any young people who showed too decided an inclination to avoid idolatry and join in any activist movement of protest became his victims (cf. 24:3–4).

Though so much responsibility is laid at Manasseh's door (cf. Jer. 15:4) for what happened to Judah, it was of course God himself who overruled the whole outcome (cf. Rom. 1:24). Manasseh '*provoked*' but it was the Lord in '*the fierceness of his great wrath*' who decided what was to happen every step of the way (23:26). It is important that we should recognise the mixed feelings that we must attribute to God if we are to think correctly about his part and his attitude in the doom that visited Judah. We cannot think of the punishment and the exile as being decreed from eternity. God's relation to Israel was basically that of faithful love (Jer. 2:2). He had had great hopes for the future of his 'marriage' to his people. He was deeply surprised and shocked that the relationship should break up. He never imagined that they should sink so low (Jer. 19:5, 7:31, 'It did not enter my mind' cf. Isa. 5:4).

When he found Baruch weeping over his own personal loss during the fall of Jerusalem he pled for some sympathy for himself in having to breakdown what he had built with such patient hope, love and skill! (Jer. 45:4–5). He called on the women to sing a dirge so that he could better express his feelings (Jer. 9:17). He entered an agonizing inner conflict with himself so that his compassion eventually prevented him from expressing the fierceness of the anger he rightly felt (Hosea 11:8–9, Isa. 54:7–8).

Josiah — Miracle, Sign and Example

It happens today in our thoroughly secularised modern society that young people can appear here and there, growing up with minds uncorrupted by the habits of thought prevalent both in the family life with which they are bound up and in the social circle in which they move. They are inclined to believe in God, and ready to follow Christ as the invitation is given to them to do so. We must always be on the alert for such miraculous occurrences, and appreciate them as signs that God has not resigned his control over the life of our community or his concern for our future.

When we read that *'Manasseh shed very much innocent blood'* (21:16) we realise that at the height of his sinister power he felt that too many young non-conformists were tending to raise their protesting voices and he tried to stamp out such conservative influence by a reign of terror. He was not successful. Isaiah had prophesied that God would not fail in that corrupt age to raise up what he called a 'remnant' (cf. Isa. 1:9, 10:21, 11:11, etc.) of the faithful, and they were always numerous enough to survive the king's attacks. Might it not be that the courage with which they endured martyrdom so deeply impressed Manasseh that it led (too late to undo the baneful effects of his life-work!) to the conversion that he is reported in the Book of Chronicles to have undergone (2 Chron. 33:10–13)?

These few found a patron and a leader in Josiah, the young grandson of Manasseh. Growing up amidst the paganism of the court of his father Amon, he took the example of King David as his ideal (22:2), and, coming to the throne at the age of eight, when he was 'still a boy', set out to purge his realm of its pagan idolatry. The witness of his presence, and the stance he took against the prevailing spirit of the age must have rallied and encouraged many around him who had become pessimistic and listless in their service of God. The remarkable persuasiveness of his power of leadership and the obvious charm of his character which marked him as endowed and blessed by God, became signs to them that God, during the gloom and deepening darkness of the days in which they lived had not forsaken his people. Here in Josiah was a token of his continuing goodness. We must regard his very appearance at this time and the whole of his consistent subsequent career as one of the outstanding miracles of God's grace and power that at critical times punctuated Israel's history. It was also a prophecy of things to come — a marvellous light shining in darkness (cf. Isa. 9:2).

His whole life-stance under these circumstances must have become in later years an example as well as a sign. At the beginning of the Babylonian captivity the conditions, under which the faithful core of believers among the exiled community found themselves, were as gloomy and unpropitious as those their fathers had faced during the reign of Manasseh. They had the same perplexing questions as they tried to work out what was happening to them under God. Had Israel itself as the people of God any hopeful future? And what were they to do if he really meant them to go ahead in his service under these new conditions? Here had been Josiah, even as a child, in the midst of the same flood of paganism as now surrounded them in Babylon, tempted in the same way to wonder if his faint efforts could count in the struggle. But he had heard the call of God and had given himself to a life of listening, obedience and toil from year to year, and under conditions which seemed to offer little hope of reward or result!

Josiah has become relevant again to many of us in our own day. Those of us who seventy years ago were brought up to believe in God and to be Christians had not much difficulty in believing that our dedicated efforts would at least in the long run bear fruit, for there was around us an almost universal conviction that the Western world would progressively come under Christian influence and that the missionary effort of the Church too would spread the reign of the Lord over human affairs. Since then there has taken place around us, irrationally and unexpectedly, the same kind of drift into a determined and aggressive paganism, shared by leadership and people, as took place in Judah towards the end of the Book of Kings. It has become an accepted cliché that we are now entering a 'post-Christian' era. We are tempted to over-estimate the difficulties in interpreting the Bible for today, and are called on to accept compromise on matters that seem to be vital to the preservation of our best traditions.

We must give some weight in our thoughts therefore to this eight year old boy who saw opening up before him a positive course in life, enabling him to stand against the drift. Like David he did not look at the difficulties, calculate the possibilities and postpone action till he had had time to think things out more thoroughly. He was helped by his respect for godly tradition. He also listened again and again for God's Word which, he finally found, came to him most powerfully through a book that had lain there at the heart of the nation's life — for years neglected.

The Book and the Purge

In the eighth year of Josiah's reign the book was discovered by the high priest during repairs in the temple. He gave it to Shaphan, the king's secretary, who when he read it decided he must take it to the palace and read it to the king. It is called here 'the *Book of the Law*' (22:8). It may have been either a copy of the Book of Deuteronomy, or have contained much of the teaching of that book. It especially emphasised God's demand that the worship of his people should be centred at one altar in the one holy place at Jerusalem. It was there they should continually seek his face and it was towards this one place that their prayers for help from any part of the land must continually be directed. God, it declared, abhorred the natural religious practices and ideas of the surrounding nations that had perverted the devotion and the minds of his people at the multitude of pagan shrines in his holy land. God hated that even his temple should be polluted and his name blasphemed by the intrusions of such idolatry into the holy place. Speedy and terrifying punishment was threatened not only for disobedience to, or deviation from, such commands, but even for tolerating such evil practices on his land.

The reading of the Book brought about within a very short period the most significant and decisive series of events within

Josiah's whole reign. The King '*tore his clothes and wept*' (22:11, 19). He was filled with intense shame and guilt over the extent to which he had allowed so many abominable practices to remain still unchallenged under his rule (see note on earlier reforms). He was terrified by the threats of the Book. He felt himself powerfully gripped by an irresistible zeal now to see that, to the utmost detail, God's word was obeyed. He sought guidance from Huldah, a prophetess. She assured him that God accepted his own individual confession of guilt and signs of repentance (22:18-20), but would never reverse his judgment on the nation as a whole. Yet Josiah followed what he regarded as a divine impulse to lead his people on a crusade for reformation. He gathered all its leaders to a solemn convention and the Book was read to them. It was a sign of the extraordinary status his personal influence had acquired during the eighteen years of his rule that the whole gathering consented to his will and entered a solemn covenant with him to purge the nation of everything displeasing to God.

The writer gives us a long and detailed description of the purge (23:4-25) because he obviously regarded it as an event of great importance. It was thorough. It tackled not only the more recent abuses by Manasseh but also those that had for centuries resisted the best efforts of the most dedicated monarchs. No offensive image or altar was left standing. No vicious religious practice was not stamped out. The religious revolution extended far into the territory of the former kingdom of Israel for the 'land' referred to in the Book was that of all the tribes. In the purge local priests were put out of their jobs and given subordinate posts in Jerusalem. Violence was at times of course involved, and there was even slaughter at Bethel where Jeroboam's altars, and the pernicious influence of his pagan priesthood, had to be destroyed. In this whole purge, the role of the king was supreme. He gave the commands and saw personally to their execution, and there is no hint of a dissentient voice. We are meant to marvel at the complete and sudden success of this purge. In the midst of what must have remained a deep and strong undercurrent of opposition and even bitter resentment, all surface protest was completely subdued. The writer intends us to read his account as if it were the catalogue of an important series of quite extraordinary miracles.

And yet at the same time we are meant to face up to the fact that the whole movement, initiated and carried out so marvellously, collapsed quite soon after it came to its climax. It did not last because God at no stage meant it to last. It was meant to take place only as a flash of extraordinary light in the surrounding gloom. God, while fulfilling his decree of judgment on this sinful nation, had wanted to make it clear that at any stage in the working out of his purposes, he had the power to restrain and direct, as he willed it, and for as long as he willed it, all human opposition. We must not be suspicious therefore of the genuineness and worth of Josiah's motives or of the nobility of his example, when we see that very soon after its spectacular success the results of his purge collapsed. After all, the momentous movement created by Jesus' miraculous ministry of preaching and healing in Galilee, seemed quite soon to collapse in failure, and the temple he so marvellously cleansed by the power of God was soon repossessed by those who had polluted it.

We must not forget, in reviewing the whole event, that the success of the purge was due not primarily to the zeal of Josiah, but to the power of the word that gripped the minds and hearts of the people when the Book was read. Many years after this, when the exiles had come home, had rebuilt the walls of the city under great difficulties and knew themselves to be in need of encouragement, cleansing and renewal, we find them again seeking guidance and inspiration from the book of Moses. They built a pulpit of wood, gathered around it and had it read and interpreted to them (Neh. 8:1-5). We find them, as they listened, strangely 'attentive' to the words, weeping for grief because they came so far short of what it commanded, and finally filled with joy as they understood its promises (Neh. 8:8-12). The final effect was again a widespread and ruthless cleansing of their national life from the abuses then prevailing in their midst. We note that this reading and interpretation of the Book took place at the heart of a service of worship. Obviously at this point in their national life they were used to such services. They had taken the Book with them to Babylon and in their need of common worship they had turned to it and to the other writings of the prophets in which they also found challenge and inspiration. It was God's purpose that a book was eventually to take the commanding place in the life and worship of the people of God in New Testament times.

The Final Phase — Tragedy and Failure?

Josiah's death brought what seemed a life full of single-hearted love for God and a career full of promise to a sudden and tragic end. The tragedy was heightened because he was still comparatively young and seemed to make himself unnecessarily the victim of idealistic folly.

The Assyrian empire was beginning to crumble. Pharaoh Necho of Egypt decided to go with his army to assist it in the struggle. On his way there he led his army through territory belonging to the former kingdom of Israel. He had no plans to make war on Judah, or disturb Josiah in any way. Yet Josiah provocatively decided to block the path of his army and challenge him to battle. No doubt the young king was encouraged and emboldened in his warlike stance, and deceived about his ability to throw out Pharaoh, by the extraordinary success he himself had just experienced with the help of God, in the reformation of his country's internal affairs. We can understand his political and religious motives for taking such a step. The Assyrians were his enemy and he wanted to block any aid that could help them. He also believed that as a descendant of the house of David he was the appointed guardian of the whole former kingdom of Israel, and that it was his sacred duty to defend it from invasion. With extreme optimism he chose the place of the conflict, Megiddo, the scene of one of Israel's past great victories against paganism (cf. Judges 5:19). Pharaoh did not want war with him, simply peaceful passage. He knew he had a great majority of men more expert in war than any in Judah. He warned Josiah, for he did not want to kill him, but the young king would not listen or yield, and the inevitable happened.

His death under these circumstances ironically ensured the immediate collapse of the reformation he had so recently brought about at home. It was Pharaoh now who had the deciding hand in the political and religious set-up in Judah. Those who favoured the continuation of Josiah's policies immediately crowned as their king his second son Jehoahaz because he knew that his elder brother would be unsympathetic to the change that his father had brought about. Pharaoh disapproving of the appointment soon dethroned him, despatched him as a prisoner to Egypt and placed on the throne the more rightful heir Eliakim whose name he changed to Jehoiakim. Under this new regime it was not long before the hidden pagan majority took control and all the former pagan practices were restored. After only two comparatively short regimes the exile finally took place.

Commentators at this point are apt to be hard on Josiah. He is alleged to have been largely himself responsible not only for the foolish sacrifice of his own life but also for the fragile and unstable nature of the reformation he toiled to bring about. Its collapse, they argue, came about because it drew its inspiration from a book of rigid and restrictive laws. It was therefore mainly legalistic and negative. Failing to inspire the common people with fresh vision and high ideals, it resorted too much to compulsion, and was wholly vitiated by the resort to violence.

We find ourselves questioning these verdicts. Certainly there was an element of folly in Josiah's sacrifice of his life. The account in Chronicles affirms that God mercifully told Pharaoh to warn him of the danger he faced in opposing him, and comments that Josiah 'did not listen to the words of Neco from the mouth of God' (2 Chron. 35:22). Yet we have to remember that it was his crusading vision of a restored Israel serving God securely and at peace within the holy land, that spurred him into his fatal action.

There can be little doubt that it was the Book itself that inspired him with this vision. Yet the book of Deuteronomy itself continually strikes a note that is evangelistic rather than legalistic. It continually appeals to each individual to turn to the Lord with all the heart and soul (Dt. 4:29–31, 6:4, cf. 2 Kings 23:25), and we do not doubt that this call, too, lay behind the motives that originally inspired the reformation and ensured its success. We believe we are correct in regarding the collapse of the reformation as having been inevitable from its start. A few years after Josiah's death God told Jeremiah that even though a Moses or a Samuel stood before him, he would not listen to their prayers or heed their efforts to save the nation (Jer. 15:1). Josiah's great effort to make an immediately successful contribution to the course of Israel's history was therefore inevitably doomed to immediate failure. But this does not mean that what he strove and prayed for so honestly was finally in vain. We can remind ourselves at this point of what Jesus warned us to expect when we work for his kingdom. We may sow good seed in our field of service. But it can happen that even before its fruit has begun to show, the growing plant can become so obscured by the apparently superior growth of evil weeds that all that is good seems to be finally blotted out. Yet the crop is still there growing in its hiddenness to be harvested in its fullness and to appear again in all its splendour in the day of final reckoning (Matt. 13:30). We are to think of both Josiah's dedicated life and the reformation he brought about as bright and marvellous lights given by the grace of God in the midst of the abounding darkness, not to be snuffed out, but merely eclipsed. His labour was not in vain.

A Labour..., 'Not in Vain'

It becomes obvious, towards the end of the Book of Kings, that God is accepting the failure of all the original plans that were in his mind when he set up a monarchy in Israel. We have had many hints of his grief and anger over such tragedy. The ensuing history, however, makes obvious his marvellous power to start again with a new design for an even better future for the people of Israel and a new plan to achieve it. When Jerusalem was falling and the monarchy was finally breaking up, he sent Jeremiah to the potter's house to watch how a vessel being made of clay was suddenly spoiled in the potter's hand. The potter did not throw away the spoiled jar, but undaunted kept it in his hands, started again kneading and 'reworked it into another vessel, as seemed good to him' (Jer. 18:1-4). We learn that God is expert at starting again in the midst of our tragic failures, and at making and carrying out new plans!

We also learn here a second important lesson: that God is expert at conserving the value and effectiveness of each worthwhile human effort that his love and grace originally inspired. Within the span of this book, how many sincere, wholly dedicated, people have we been reading about — 'prophets, kings, rank and file men and women'! They poured out their lives sometimes with excruciating sacrifice and suffering. Many of them were as deeply involved as Josiah here seemed to be in failure and tragedy, sometimes happening at some crisis in their lives, sometimes at the time of their deaths. They are written about, however, in such a way that we are aware of God's close fellowship with them in their afflictions, and of his appreciation of the worth of their devotion and doings. Because the sacrifice of their hearts and lives registered in this way before God we know that it is treasured forever in his mind, and that nothing of the contribution of their lives to his kingdom was or is, in vain. We have evidence, too, that at the height of their desolation they were conscious that God himself was their witness, valued what they did and would never allow it to go to waste. We have suggested that the triumphal ending to the lives both of Elijah and Elisha, both of whose life-work eventually failed, are an indication of the validity of this interpretation of the stories about them. Jeremiah, who understood well the ways and power of God, admired Josiah, and was confident that his life counted. To those who were tempted to regard his end as tragic, he wrote, 'do not weep for him' (Jer. 22:10). There is a memorable utterance in one of the Psalms where the writer expresses his confidence in vivid terms:

> 'You have kept count of my tossings;
> put my tears in your bottle.
> Are they not in your record?'
>   (Ps 56:8. In many translations 'record' = 'book').

A 'bottle' for tears, there with God, so that no suffering undergone for the sake of righteousness will ever be heedlessly forgotten! A book to be opened before him when everything is put right at his judgment seat! It discounts all false rumour and misses nothing out!

If all this is implied simply in the style and tone of Old Testament utterance and story, it is made quite explicit in the New Testament as one of the central truths of the Gospel. The New Testament disciples had their failures and tragedies. Even then parental love was being poured out on worthless and irresponsible children, good enterprises involving enormous sacrifice could collapse in failure and sometimes in disgrace. 'Your labour is not in vain in the Lord' wrote Paul to them. He wrote this at the end of 1 Corinthians 15, a chapter on the message of the resurrection of Jesus, raised from the dead by God! He had died on Good Friday — a failure, despised and rejected, slandered and hated, his friends and followers in hiding and tempted to despair. But God the righteous One was there in full control. In his sight the very failure and agony of his Son had been the climax of the one perfect life on earth that he had been planning and seeking for, since the foundation of the world. Jesus' resurrection is the final word of assurance from God to falling and struggling believers today that none who has ever looked to him and now lives in him inspired by his power and example, will ever go unrecognised by him, and that no deed done in his name, however great or small will ever go unrewarded.

Notes

On Josiah's Early Reform

While the Book of Kings gives us no information about Josiah's reforming activity during the first eighteen years of his life, the Book of Chronicles tells us that from the eighth year of his reign, while he was still a boy, he began to seek God, and that four years later he began to purge Judah and Jerusalem (2 Chron. 34:3). These reforms extending over a period of six years are described as devastatingly thorough, cleansing religious practice over the whole land of what savoured of Baalism and Assyrian influence, and they extended even into Northern Israel territory. It was at the close of this period that the book was found. It is to be noted that the international situation — the waning power of Assyria — during this period, would be favourable for such reforms. J. G. McConville thinks that the chronicler has 'preserved an account of the matter that conveys more precisely what actually happened', and that the author of Kings wanted to stress the penitence of Josiah after reading the Book (Chronicles, p. 256).

The 'Book of the Law'
The fear that possessed Josiah and the nature of the further reforms which he immediately put into effect, have led to the conclusion that the 'Book' found in the temple at least contained important passages of warning and instructions from our present Book of Deuteronomy. It contains the threats that would inspire Josiah's fear and its requirements correspond in many details to reforms that obviously dominated Josiah's mind as he set out on his subsequent crusade. Moreover its description of the passover seems to have guided him in the way he celebrated that festival. That the book seems to have been read at one sitting, and, indeed twice in one day, means that it could not have been the whole law (though 2 Chron. 34:18 could imply that only sections of the 'Book' were read). How the Book got where it was has given rise to speculation. It has even been suggested that it was a recent pious fraud, and that Hilkiah was merely pretending to have found it. Moses is said in Deuteronomy to have commanded that a copy of the law should be kept alongside the Ark in the temple (Deut. 31:34ff.), and it was a custom also to deposit valuable records and documents in the foundations of buildings.

On 23:15–18. This incident refers to a prophecy made by an unnamed 'man of God' in the reign of Jeroboam I, in judgment against his apostasy (cf. 1 Kings 13:2). When the 'man of God' was wronged by a local prophet, and slain by a lion on his journey home, the local prophet was led to repent for his shameful treatment of a colleague, ensured his honorable burial, at Bethel, and expressed the desire to be buried in the same grave, confident that God would honour his prophecy (see my *Readings in 1 Kings* pp. 86–90).

On 23:21–23 — Josiah's Passover. It is emphasised in the Chronicles account of the passover held in Josiah's time that 'no passover like it had been kept in Israel since the days of

Josiah

the prophet Samuel' (2 Chron. 35:18). There are striking differences between this passover (closely similar to that prescribed in Deuteronomy) and the kind of celebration prescribed in Exodus, chapter 12. The latter takes place within the heart of the life of each family, each household making its own sacrifice at the appointed time. It could be celebrated where the community were on the move, e.g. under Joshua it took place in the plains of Jericho (Joshua 5:10f.). As prescribed in the Book of Deuteronomy, however, (cf. especially Deut. 15) it could take place only at a central sanctuary in which the lambs were meant to be slain. Hezekiah's great renewal celebration of the feast was centred in Jerusalem but the Levites sacrificed the lambs by families and they themselves were not in a state of Levitical purity. In the celebration ordered by Josiah everything was more in accordance with the ideal set down in the Book.

Points for further thought and discussion
We have argued in this study that after the fateful reign of Ahaz no hope remained of an enduring monarchy within the kingdom of Judah. We are meant to notice how God (slowly) allowed its history to work itself out as it moved towards the final collapse of the regime. After Ahaz there appeared Manasseh and Jeroboam both of whom displayed even worse features than Ahaz. And Hezekiah and Josiah, better than any predecessor, also appeared. Think of Jesus' parable of the Weeds and the Wheat (Mat. 13:24–30, 37–43) which suggests that as periodic conflicts between good and evil move to their climax, good gets better, and evil gets worse. Might this be a clue to understanding our perplexing state in the conflict between Christianity and paganism which seems to be taking place in the Western world today?

Manasseh used tyrannical power to compel the people to conform to his religious programme. He also, we are told, seduced them to do evil (21:9 R.S.V.). Today we are very conscious of having to safeguard democratic freedom against tyranny by defending civil liberties. Think of how even more powerfully around us people are being strangely and subtly deceived and drawn into perverse thought, practice and worship by the seductive power of evil. Study John 12:31–33. Was Jesus promising to liberate from the seductive power of evil when he said that 'now' the 'prince of this world' would be judged and 'cast out' of his place of power over the inner hearts of men and women? What does it mean that we ourselves have to 'lift him up' so that this can happen?

Here is an occasion when the (very!) lengthy reading of Holy Scripture, without any immediate comment, conveyed its own message with great power to those who listened. Have you yourself experienced being held, and illuminated in your mind by simply hearing long passages of scripture read in this way? Have the traditional churches been correct in ensuring through prescribed lectionaries that such disciplined reading of scripture takes a prominent place in worship? Do we sometimes rob our people of an important source of blessing and illumination, by neglecting such discipline?

When a class was asked to define 'repentance' one pupil answered, 'Being sorry for your sin'. Another corrected him, saying, 'Being sorry enough to quit'. Josiah certainly made every effort to quit sinning, but he was inspired to do so by intensely felt grief (22:19) and fear. Read Paul's description of how 'godly grief' led to repentance (2 Cor. 7:9–15) suggesting that grief was an essential ingredient of repentance. The woman who had sinned much, wept much (Luke 7:36–50). Zacchaeus did not seem to show much emotion (Luke 19:1–9). What do you think?

Josiah's irresponsible campaign against Pharaoh Necho in Israel is a reminder to us that as happened even in the case of David, God does not prevent tragedy happening to us when we foolishly court it. Josiah is blamed for his irresponsible decision. An English preacher published a sermon on this tragic end of Josiah entitled 'Even Mistakes Punished'. Think over the relevance of such a message for us today. Think of Paul's injunction to 'fear and tremble' as we work out our own salvation (Phil. 2:12) and Jesus' frequent call to us to 'Watch'.

EPILOGUE
2 Kings 23:31–25:30

The Narrative

The writer, in this last section of his book seems to have no other purpose than to give as condensed a record as possible of the historical facts as they succeeded one another. He describes the invasions of 597 when many of the important citizens were taken into exile, and the further siege and fall of the city in 587 with the destruction of the temple. He is concerned that we should know the fate of the temple vessels, and he summarises the tragic history of the remnant which forced Gedaliah to accompany them into Egypt.

Few biographical details are given of the last four kings. Jehoahaz was allowed only three months rule till his deposition by Pharaoh Necho. Our historian, without giving us any detail, condemns him for reverting to the evil of his ancestors, and Jeremiah utters a few words of lament for him as a tragic and hopeless figure, doomed to die in his exile (Jer. 22:10–12).

It is to the Book of Jeremiah that we would have to turn for the fascinating and detailed stories first about Jehoiakim's vicious hatred and contempt for the prophet and the Word of God, and then Zedekiah's pathetic anxiety to consult and protect him from enraged public opinion. All that the writer of Kings tells us is that both monarchs by their foolish and vacillating conduct of foreign affairs needlessly incurred the anger of the one man they should have respected. Jehoiakim had died before Nebuchadnezzar reached the city in 597 and his son Jehoiachin had reigned there for three months. This unfortunate king was taken to Babylon along with his mother. We are told of him too, that he 'did what was evil in the sight of the Lord just as his father had done' (24:9).

In the year 562, however, after years of imprisonment he was, at the beginning of the reign of Evil-merodach the successor to Nebuchadnezzar released from prison, and given even honorable treatment for the rest of his life. Skinner well sums up the significance of this event. 'It must have excited the liveliest expectations in the Jewish community. The bestowal of royal honours on their king was at once a recognition of their nationality and, from a higher point of view, a pledge of Yahweh's continued favour to the dynasty of David, round which the messianic hope had entwined itself.'

www.ingramcontent.com/pod-product-compliance
Lightning Source LLC
Chambersburg PA
CBHW060605230426
43670CB00011B/1982